One-Pot Dishes for Every Season

One-Pot Dishes for Every Season

Over 100 delicious recipes

Norma Miller

Skyhorse Publishing

Skyhorse Publishing books may be purchased in bulk at special discounts
for sales promotion, corporate gifts, fund-raising, or educational purposes.
Special editions can also be created to specifications. For details, contact
the Special Sales Department, Skyhorse Publishing,
555 Eighth Avenue, Suite 903, New York, NY 10018 or
info@skyhorsepublishing.com.

www.skyhorsepublishing.com

10 9 8 7 6 5 4 3 2 1

Library of Congress Cataloging-in-Publication Data
Miller, Norma, 1949–
One-pot dishes for every season : over 100 delicious recipes / by Norma Miller.
p. cm.
Includes index.
ISBN 978-1-61608-016-7 (pb : alk. paper)
1. One-dish meals. 2. Casserole cookery. I. Title.
TX840.O53M55 2010
641.8'21--dc22
2010008922

Printed in China

Contents

Introduction

DISHES prepared with just one pan and meals made with fresh in-season ingredients − these are the two themes I have woven together within the covers of this book.

One-pot cooking is simple, effective and economical. Seasonal produce is good value, healthy and full of flavour. With over one hundred recipes, *One-Pot Dishes for Every Season* should inspire and encourage you to create wholesome and stylish food based on the very best each season has to offer.

All the recipes are new, they have been designed specifically for cooking at home, and the preparation and cooking processes for each recipe are straightforward and easy to follow. To make things even easier, there are plenty of serving suggestions and hints and tips to go with the recipes.

Recently there has been a resurgence of interest in home cooking, and it is fashionable once again to 'eat-out-in'. There is much more enthusiasm and excitement these days around the idea of cooking from scratch. This has a great deal to do with our increasing knowledge about the foodstuffs we are buying and consuming, and our desire to eat more sensibly, healthily and economically. And a host of influences and trends can be introduced as well − creative, inspirational and aspirational ideas drawing variously on global, local, home-grown and specialist produce.

With all these exciting connections, a wonderful choice of freshly-cooked meals is at your fingertips. Ideal for modern lifestyles, these recipes are fun and fulfilling, adventurous and achievable.

One-Pot Dishes

S O WHAT counts as a 'pot' in a one-pot dish? It can be any item you select from your kitchen cupboard in which to cook your chosen meal. It can be a roasting tin or an oven-proof casserole for the oven, a saucepan, frying pan, steamer or wok for the hob, or any suitable dish for the microwave. And then you can grill, boil, fry, roast, bake, stir-fry or microwave. So there is plenty of variety in terms of equipment used and method employed, all within the 'one-pot' formula.

There are practical advantages too. One-pot recipes save energy (whether using the microwave, hob or grill), they take up less space, reduce effort, streamline the cooking process and cut down on the washing up.

Every Season

FOR ME the great attraction of the seasonal approach to cooking is the way you can feel you are joining in with the rhythms of nature. Fruit, vegetables, herbs and produce of many kinds have their optimal seasons when flavours and textures are at their most vibrant, tender, succulent, rich or ripe.

Each season has its own chapter, with the ingredients highlighted in each recipe reflecting seasonal availability, freshness and variety. In combination, ingredients selected in this way provide signature dishes for their respective seasons.

Of course, around the country seasons vary slightly from place to place, and produce in peak condition can overlap at the beginning or end of a season, often depending on where you live. Although some things like potatoes and cabbages are available all year round, the varieties change throughout the year, and it is well worth looking out for the different types on display and sampling as many as you can.

It is always a good idea to buy locally from your butcher, fishmonger and greengrocer, from street markets and farmers' markets, or even direct from local producers. You may be part of a 'veg-box' scheme, and there are plenty of pick-your-own farms. And if you have the space, why not grow as much produce as you can in your own garden or back yard? I find I can grow 'cut-and-come' salad leaves throughout most of the year – from spring to the first frosts later in the year – outside, without heating being needed.

If you travel, watch out for any in-season produce wherever you find yourself – this may be something ripening earlier or later than you are used to, or an unfamiliar regional variety. I know I find it a joy to snap up a treat like this, and then think up ideas about how to use it while hurrying back to my kitchen.

The secret is to let yourself be inspired by the best of whatever is available. When you think of cooking, think seasonal.

The Recipes

WITHIN each seasonal chapter the recipes roughly follow a sequence – soups, light meals, main meals (vegetarian, fish, meat, poultry and game), then pasta, noodles and beans, and finally desserts. In some cases I recommend salsas, salads, breads, sauces or other accompaniments so that the recipes become rounded meals.

Mostly the recipes serve four or two people, but some serve six. They all use fresh seasonal ingredients, to which I add a mix of store-cupboard and canned foods. The recipes are often adaptable and you can easily substitute interchangeable ingredients as you wish. Apart from the 'one-pot', I've kept the use of other equipment when needed for the preparation stages to a minimum.

Hints & Tips

▶ For convenience, the recipe ingredients are listed in the order in which they are used. Though they are given in imperial as well as metric, UK readers will find the metric measurements easier.

▶ When measuring volumes of liquid, US readers should follow the cup quantities since UK (not US) pints are used in the recipes.

▶ If shop-bought pastry is not available, use the equivalent weight of home-made pastry.

▶ You will find both the British and the American names for many common ingredients throughout the book.

▶ Most of the recipes can produce extra servings by doubling the quantity of ingredients – but make sure this increased volume still goes into the one pot.

▶ Is your 'one-pot' pan large enough? It's usually best to think big. Use a wide, shallow pan or a wok, if appropriate, or for cooking pasta and noodles, a deep pan with plenty of room.

▶ Sometimes I use a stick blender for whizzing soups into chunky or smooth blends – as an alternative you could use a food processor.

▶ For the recipes cooked in an oven, the oven is pre-heated. If you have a fan oven, pre-heating may not be needed, so check your instruction book.

▶ If a recipe uses a microwave oven then the recipes have been tested with a wattage of 700–800W.

▶ My store-cupboard always contains canned tomatoes, a selection of canned beans, and small jars of pastes that are so quick and convenient – garlic, curry and chilli. Also a wide selection of spices and spice mixes.

▶ Another favourite store-cupboard ingredient is vegetable bouillon powder. I particularly like using this because it's granular, and you can spoon out as much or as little as you want.

▶ All spoon measures are level unless otherwise stated.

▶ Salt is kept to a minimum. Instead I prefer to source good quality ingredients that have bags of flavour. Often just a handful of freshly chopped herbs is all you need to boost flavour.

▶ Some recipes contain eggs – please remember that it may be advisable to avoid eating eggs if you are pregnant, elderly, very young or sick.

▶ If you are preparing food for someone who has a food allergy be sure to study the list of ingredients carefully.

▶ Some recipes contain fresh chillies. Do take care when preparing them and remember to wash your hands thoroughly afterwards. Better still, wear rubber gloves while handling them.

Spring

S PRING is such an optimistic season. The days begin to lengthen, green shoots begin to appear, and you start to look forward to good things coming up.

In cooking as in painting, restricting your palette of flavours and colours can often bring about excellent results. The tastes of spring are fresh, lively and delicate; just think of the first flush of young salad leaves, leafy greens, young beans and herbs. Spring colours are bright and cheerful – young carrots and mange-touts, rhubarb and edible flowers. And what better to go with delicious seasonal lamb, pigeon or duck than tender young asparagus, young courgettes with their flowers still attached, spinach, watercress or pak choi.

To see how much of spring you can get onto your plate, just try out some of the recipes in this chapter, such as Asparagus and Chervil Omelette (page 21), Chorizo, Broad Bean and Bulgur Wheat Salad (page 32), Pigeon Breasts with Red Chard and Polenta (page 36) or Hot Creamy Rhubarb Fool with Maple Syrup (page 53).

Spring Vegetables and Rice Soup

A bright colourful soup. Spring is the time of year for young tiny courgettes (zucchini) – look for those with their bright yellow edible flowers still attached.

Serves 4

4 mini courgettes (zucchini) with flowers

1 medium leek

1 garlic clove

Small piece of fresh root ginger

1 red chilli (see page 13)

175 g/6 oz mange-touts

2 tbsp sunflower oil

2 tbsp vegetable bouillon powder

4 heaped tbsp cooked white or brown rice

Freshly milled salt and pepper

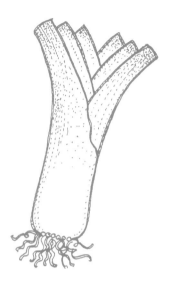

▶ Put the kettle on to boil. Remove the courgette (zucchini) flowers, trim and thinly slice the leek and courgettes (zucchini). Finely chop the garlic, ginger and chilli. Cut the mange-touts into strips diagonally. Grate the garlic, ginger and chilli, keeping it separate.

▶ Heat the oil in a large saucepan and add the leek, courgettes (zucchini) and garlic. Cook gently for about 5 minutes, stirring occasionally, until beginning to soften but not brown.

▶ Pour 850 ml/1½ pints/3½ cups boiling water (from the kettle) into the pan and stir in the bouillon powder, ginger, chilli, mange-touts and rice. Bring just to the boil, reduce the heat and cook gently for 8 minutes. Stir in the courgette (zucchini) flowers and cook for a further few minutes.

▶ Season if necessary and serve immediately.

Tomato, Chilli and Nettle Soup

*Nettles are easy to find to make a tasty soup.
Wear gloves to pick the new fresh nettle tops and
carefully shake to remove any insects.
Mozzarella cheese melts quickly in the piping
hot soup. Serve with bread or nachos.*

Serves 4

4 large handfuls of nettle tops or spinach leaves
1 large red onion
350 g/12 oz tomatoes
1 lemon
55 g/2 oz mozzarella cheese
1 tbsp sunflower oil
400 ml/14 fl oz/1²/₃ cups vegetable or chicken stock
Freshly milled salt and black pepper

1. ▶ Thoroughly wash the nettle tops or spinach leaves in plenty of cold water. Finely chop the onion. Roughly chop the tomatoes, discarding any tough cores. Slice the lemon in half, squeeze the juice from one half and cut the other half into thin slices. Tear the mozzarella cheese into small pieces.

2. ▶ Heat the oil in a medium pan and add the chopped onion. Cook over a gentle heat for about 5 minutes until softened and lightly browned.

3. ▶ Stir in the tomatoes, stock and lemon juice. Bring to the boil, reduce the heat and cook for 5–8 minutes. Tip in the leaves and cook for 6–8 minutes until wilted and cooked through.

4. ▶ Using a stick blender, whiz until fairly smooth. If the soup is too thick, thin with a little boiling water and season to taste.

5. ▶ Reheat, pour into bowls and top each with a lemon slice and scatter over some mozzarella cheese.

Mussels with Tomatoes and Fennel

Serve with plenty of fresh crusty bread and wedges of lemon.

*Serves 4 as a starter
or 2 as a main course*

1.8 kg/4 lb mussels in their shells
3 shallots
2 garlic cloves
6 tomatoes
4 tbsp chopped fresh fennel leaves
4 tbsp chopped fresh parsley
1 tbsp olive oil
150 ml/¼ pint/⅔ cup fish or vegetable stock
150 ml/¼ pint/⅔ cup dry white wine
Freshly milled black pepper

1. Scrub the mussels, discarding any with broken shells and any that do not close when given a sharp knock. Pull off the beards (the black hairy tufts hanging out of the shell).

2. Finely chop the shallots. Finely chop or crush the garlic. Roughly chop the tomatoes and finely chop the fennel and parsley.

3. Put the oil, shallots and garlic into a very large pan and heat through without allowing the garlic to brown.

4. Tip the mussels into the pan, add the stock, white wine, tomatoes, a little black pepper and half of the chopped fennel and parsley. Cover with a lid and cook quickly for 4–5 minutes, shaking the pan occasionally, until the mussels have opened (discard any that haven't).

5. Stir in the remaining chopped herbs and serve immediately.

Asparagus and Chervil Omelette

Rather than cut the woody end of asparagus spears, bend the end – it will snap finding its natural breaking point. Chervil adds a delicate hint of anise. Serve with a crisp leafy green salad with edible flowers.

Serves 2

6 asparagus spears

1 small red onion

5 large eggs

2 tsp freshly chopped parsley

4 tsp freshly chopped chervil

Freshly milled black pepper

Butter for frying

Green salad, to serve

1▶ Trim the 'woody' part from the base of the asparagus spears. Cut each diagonally into six pieces. Finely chop the onion. Break the eggs into a bowl and add 2 tbsp cold water, the parsley and the chervil. Season with pepper.

2▶ Heat a medium non-stick frying pan, add a little butter and when melted stir in the onion and asparagus pieces. Cook for a few minutes, stirring occasionally until cooked and golden.

3▶ Pour the egg mixture over and cook gently, drawing the set mixture away from the sides of the pan to the centre (the liquid egg will run and fill the gaps – don't stir too much otherwise you will have scrambled eggs).

4▶ When the omelette is soft on the top and golden underneath, brown quickly under a hot grill (broiler).

5▶ Cut in half and serve immediately.

Sardines in Vine Leaves

Packs of edible flowers are available in some stores — they must be free from pesticides. Nasturtiums taste peppery and violets taste a little bit like mushrooms.

Serves 2–4

12–15 large fresh vine leaves or 125 g/4½ oz
  preserved vine leaves
1 large lemon
Large bunch of dill leaves
Large handful of edible flowers
2 spring onions (scallions)
12 sardines, gutted
Freshly milled salt and black pepper
Olive oil
Two large handfuls of small salad leaves

1. ▶ Put the kettle on to boil. If using preserved vine leaves, rinse several times in cold water to remove the brine and drain. If using fresh leaves, trim the stalks and put into a bowl. Pour over boiling water (from the kettle) and leave for 30 seconds until the leaves have wilted. Drain and rinse in cold water until cold. Dry on kitchen paper.

2. ▶ Finely grate the rind from the lemon, cut in half and squeeze the juice. Chop the dill leaves. Pull the leaves from the edible flowers. Thinly slice the spring onions (scallions).

3. ▶ Wash the sardines and pat dry with kitchen paper. Open them out and sprinkle a little lemon rind, dill and seasoning along the fish and fold back.

4. ▶ Open out the vine leaves – if small overlap two or three. Place a sardine in the centre of each leaf and wrap the leaf around like a parcel.

5. ▶ Brush with oil and cook under a hot grill (broiler) for a few minutes on either side, brushing with more oil if needed, until cooked through – or cook in a wide frying pan.

6. ▶ Pour the lemon juice into a small jug and stir in the lemon rind, 3 tbsp olive oil and a little seasoning. Pile the salad leaves, spring onions (scallions), remaining dill and flowers in a bowl and drizzle over the lemon juice dressing. Serve with the cooked sardines.

Vegetarian Biriani

Carnivores can add pieces of boneless chicken, beef, lamb or pork at the start and cook in the hot oil until cooked through. Serve with naan breads, poppadoms, yogurt, chutney and pickles.

Serves 4

1 onion

3 carrots

1 small leek

1 garlic clove

150 g/5½ oz French beans

3 tomatoes

Small bunch of coriander

2 tbsp olive oil

Handful of sultanas

1 tbsp curry paste, your own choice of 'heat'

300 ml/½ pint/1¼ cups vegetable stock

500 g/1 lb 2 oz cooked ready-to-eat basmati rice

55 g/2 oz/¼ cup toasted flaked almonds

1. Finely chop the onion and carrots and thinly slice the leek. Slice or crush the garlic. Trim the beans and cut each into three. Roughly chop the tomatoes and finely chop the coriander.

2. Heat the oil in large non-stick pan and cook the onion and carrots until softened but not browned. Add the leek and stir in the tomatoes, beans, sultanas, curry paste, garlic and stock. Cook for 6–8 minutes until the vegetables are tender.

3. Stir the rice into the pan and cook for 3–5 minutes, stirring constantly to prevent it from sticking, until the rice is piping hot. Stir in the coriander and almonds and serve immediately.

Spring Vegetables with Seeds

A rainbow-coloured dish of young tiny spring vegetables.

Serves 4

900 g/2 lb selection of mini vegetables, such as turnips, leeks,
  sweetcorn, carrots, courgettes (zucchini)
25 g/1 oz/2 tbsp butter
1 tbsp olive oil
1 tbsp yellow mustard seeds
1 tbsp sesame seeds
1 tbsp onion seeds
150 ml/¼ pint/²/₃ cup vegetable stock
3 tbsp sweet chilli sauce
2 large handfuls of spinach leaves
Freshly milled salt and black pepper

1. Trim the vegetables, leaving the leaves attached. Cut in half only if they are large.

2. Heat the butter and oil in a frying pan or wok. Stir in the mustard, sesame and onion seeds and heat until they begin to 'pop'.

3. Put the mini vegetables into the pan and turn in the spices and oil until starting to brown. Reduce the heat, pour in the stock, bring just to the boil and cook for 3–4 minutes until the vegetables are tender. Reduce the heat and stir in the chilli sauce and the spinach leaves. Cook for a further 3–4 minutes until the spinach has wilted. Season if necessary and serve immediately.

Goat's Cheese and Courgette Tart

Choose a firm goat's cheese to crumble rather than a very soft one.
Serve with mixed salad.

Serves 4–6

1 small red pepper
6 cherry tomatoes
2 mini courgettes (zucchini)
2 mini leeks
6 sprigs of oregano
2 medium eggs
100 g/3½ oz goat's cheese
2 tbsp chopped walnuts
Freshly milled salt and black pepper
375 g/13 oz packet ready-rolled shortcrust pastry
2 tsp olive oil

1. Preheat the oven to 190°C, 375°F, Fan 175°C, Gas 5. Cut the pepper in half, remove the stalk and seeds and cut into thin strips. Halve the tomatoes and cut each courgette (zucchini) and leek into three. Pull the leaves from the sprigs of oregano.

2. Lightly beat the eggs in a bowl, crumble in the goat's cheese and stir in the walnuts and a little seasoning, but leave the mix lumpy, not a smooth paste.

3. Unroll the pastry and use to line a deep 20 cm/8 inch flan ring. Trim any excess pastry. Pour the egg mixture into the flan case and arrange the vegetables on top.

4. Brush or drizzle the oil over the vegetables and scatter over the oregano leaves.

5. Put into the hot oven and cook for 30–40 minutes until the pastry is golden, the filling is set and the vegetables are tender.

Saffron Rice with Mussels and Prawns (Shrimps)

A spicy tasty meal with lots of ingredients which all disappear into one pot. Serve with lemon wedges. For special occasions add a few scallops, halved if large.

Serves 4

1 large onion
3 garlic cloves
1 red chilli (see page 13)
Small piece of fresh ginger
Small bunch of parsley
1 lemon
350 g/12 oz mussels in their shells
2–3 tbsp olive oil
350 g/12 oz paella rice or risotto rice
1.2 litres/2 pints/5 cups chicken or vegetable stock
Large pinch of saffron threads
Freshly milled black pepper
150 g/5 oz peas
200 g/7 oz raw shelled prawns (shrimps)
12–16 whole raw prawns (shrimps) in their shells

1. Finely chop the onion and crush the garlic. Halve the chilli, remove the seeds and thinly shred. Grate the ginger. Finely chop the parsley. Grate the rind from the lemon, cut in half and squeeze the juice. Scrub the mussels, discarding any with broken shells and any that do not close when given a sharp knock. Pull off the beards (the black hairy tufts hanging out of the shell).

2. Put the oil, onion and garlic into a large, shallow pan and cook gently for 5–10 minutes, stirring occasionally, until softened but not browned.

3. Add the rice and cook, stirring, for 1–2 minutes.

4. Stir in the stock, lemon rind and juice, saffron threads, chilli, ginger and black pepper, and bring just to the boil. Reduce the heat and cook very gently (uncovered and preferably without stirring) for about 20 minutes or until the rice is just cooked and the liquid has been absorbed.

5. Add the peas, mussels, and the shelled and unshelled prawns (shrimps). Continue cooking for about 5 minutes or until cooked through and piping hot. Discard any unopened shells.

6. Stir in the chopped parsley and serve immediately.

Thai Coconut Sauce Fish Balls

If you're short of time, cut the fish into small bite-size pieces instead of making the fish balls.

Serves 4

2 spring onions (scallions)
Small bunch of chives
6 Chinese leaves
Small bunch of coriander
1 red chilli (see page 13)
Small piece of fresh ginger
300 g/10½ oz skinless, boneless white fish fillet
1 medium egg yolk
2 tsp Thai green curry paste
300 ml/½ pint/1¼ cups chicken stock
150 ml/¼ pint/²⁄₃ cup coconut milk
2 tbsp fish sauce
Freshly milled salt and black pepper

1. Thinly slice one of the spring onions (scallions), the chives and the Chinese leaves. Finely chop the coriander. Halve the chilli, remove the seeds and thinly slice. Grate the ginger.

2. Roughly chop the fish and the other spring onion (scallion) and put into a food processor with the egg and 1 tsp of the curry paste. Process for a few seconds until coarsely chopped rather than a paste.

3. With wetted hands, shape heaped teaspoons of the mixture into balls. Chill for 10 minutes.

4. Pour the stock, coconut milk and fish sauce into a wide shallow pan. Stir in the chilli, ginger, chives and remaining Thai curry paste. Bring just to the boil, reduce the heat to a simmer, add the fish balls, a few at a time, and cook for 2 minutes until set and cooked. Lift from the pan with a slotted spoon.

5. Stir in the sliced spring onion (scallion), Chinese leaves and coriander. Bring to the boil and cook for 3–4 minutes. Stir in the fish balls and heat until piping hot and cooked through. Season if necessary and serve immediately.

Chorizo, Broad Bean and Bulgur Wheat Salad

This is delicious served as a meal on its own or with a few salad leaves, natural yogurt and hot breads.

Serves 4

175 g/6 oz/1½ cups bulgur wheat

1 red onion

Small bunch of mint

Small bunch of parsley

1 lemon

8 tomatoes, various colours

85 g/3 oz/¾ cup stoned (pitted) black olives

200 g/7 oz piece of chorizo or spicy sausage

4 tbsp olive oil

½ tsp ground cumin

Freshly milled salt and black pepper

200 g/7 oz shelled young broad beans

55 g/2 oz/¼ cup pine nuts

1. Put the kettle on to boil. Tip the bulgur wheat into a bowl, cover with boiling water (from the kettle) and leave to stand for 35–45 minutes. Thinly slice the onion. Finely chop the mint and parsley. Grate the rind from the lemon, cut in half and squeeze the juice. Cut the tomatoes in half, remove the seeds and finely chop. Cut the olives in half. Thinly slice the chorizo.

2. Pour the oil into a large bowl and stir in the chopped herbs, ground cumin, lemon rind and juice, tomatoes and olives.

3. Drain the bulgur wheat in a fine sieve or colander lined with a tea-towel. Press to remove as much of the water as possible.

4. Stir the grains into the dressing and season if necessary.

5. Put the broad beans into a saucepan and pour over boiling water. Cook for 10 minutes until tender, then drain. Whilst the beans are warm, peel away the skins to reveal the bright green bean underneath (if you have time).

6. Wipe the pan with kitchen paper then heat without adding any oil. Cook the chorizo and onion until golden, add the pine nuts for a few seconds until 'toasted'.

7. Stir the broad beans, hot chorizo, onion and pine nuts into the salad. Stir well and serve warm or cold.

Lemon Chicken in a Crunchy Peanut Sauce

This dish works equally well with turkey.

Serves 4

1 small onion
1 garlic clove
1 lemon
Small piece of spring cabbage
1 cucumber
2 carrots
4 skinless, boneless chicken breasts
1 bay leaf
6 black peppercorns
2 tsp chicken bouillon powder
3 tbsp crunchy peanut butter
1 tbsp light soy sauce

1▶ Put the kettle on to boil. Halve the onion and crush the garlic. Cut the lemon in half and squeeze the juice. Finely shred the cabbage. Halve the cucumber, scrape out the seeds and cut into thin strips. Cut the carrots into matchstick sized pieces.

2▶ Put the chicken into a large pan, add the onion, bay leaf, peppercorns, bouillon powder and lemon juice. Pour over 300ml/½ pint/1¼ cups boiling water, cover and cook for 25–35 minutes until cooked through. Stir in the carrot strips and cabbage for the last 5 minutes.

3▶ Lift the chicken and carrot from the pan and keep warm. With a slotted spoon remove the onion, bay leaf and peppercorns from the liquid and discard.

4▶ To the remaining liquid stir in the peanut butter, soy sauce and garlic. Cut the chicken into thin slices. Heat the sauce until bubbling and carefully stir in the carrot, cabbage, cucumber and chicken. Cook until the chicken is piping hot and serve immediately.

35

Pigeon Breasts with Red Chard and Polenta

Wood pigeon breasts are very lean and tender with a fine flavour.

Serves 2

6 wood pigeon breasts
1 shallot
Sprig of thyme
2 tbsp red wine
2 tsp liquid chicken stock
Freshly milled black pepper
2 tbsp olive oil
250 g/9 oz ready-made polenta
8 walnut pieces
200 g/7 oz small red chard leaves

1 ▶ Wash the pigeon breasts and dry with kitchen paper. Finely chop the shallot, pull the leaves from the thyme stalk and put into a large bowl. Stir in the wine, stock, black pepper and 1 tbsp of the oil.

2 ▶ Turn the pigeon breasts in the marinade, cover and chill for 30 minutes, or 2 hours if there's time. Lift the pigeon breasts from the marinade.

3 ▶ Cut the polenta into six slices or chip shapes.

4 ▶ Heat a wide shallow pan, preferably non-stick, until hot. Put the polenta and pigeon breasts into the pan, cooking and turning the polenta until browned and the pigeon breasts for 5–6 minutes, turning once until sealed and browned.

5 ▶ Remove the polenta from the pan, pour the marinade over the meat and add the walnuts. Cook for a further 5 minutes until the pigeon is pink inside or a little longer if you prefer it cooked throughout.

6 ▶ Lift the cooked pigeon breasts onto a plate, cover and leave to rest for 2–3 minutes. Return the polenta to the pan, add the chard leaves and cook for 2–3 minutes until lightly cooked.

7 ▶ Serve immediately.

Roasted Parmesan and Cumin Chicken with Beetroots (Beets)

A whole roast dinner from the one pan.
It is also delicious made with duck.

Serves 4

4 boneless, skinless chicken breasts
2 potatoes
2 small onions
4 small beetroots (beets)
Small bunch of oregano
Small bunch of parsley
1 tbsp olive oil
2 medium egg whites
2 tbsp grated Parmesan cheese
3 tbsp cornmeal
2 tsp ground cumin
Freshly milled salt and black pepper

1. Preheat the oven to 190°C, 375°F, Fan 175°C, Gas 5.

2. Cut each chicken breast into three long thin pieces. Cut the potatoes and onions into wedges. Quarter the beetroots (beets). Pull the leaves from the oregano and finely chop the parsley.

3. Pour the oil into a large bowl and stir in half of the oregano leaves and parsley.

4. Lightly beat the egg whites in another bowl. On a large plate mix together the Parmesan cheese, cornmeal, cumin and a little seasoning. Dip the chicken in the egg white and then into the coating, pressing it onto the chicken.

5. Put the potatoes and onions into a large roasting tin. Stir the beetroot (beet) pieces into the oil and spoon into the tin. Spread to a single layer. Put into the hot oven and cook for 10 minutes. Add the chicken and cook for 20 minutes or until the chicken is golden brown and cooked through.

6. Sprinkle over the remaining herbs and serve piping hot.

Trout with Shredded Vegetables

Ask the fishmonger to clean the fish. Sorrel leaves look similar to spinach leaves and have a sharp lemon flavour.

Serves 4

55 g/2 oz/¼ cup butter

2 red onions

3 carrots

4 courgettes (zucchini) – 2 yellow, 2 green

3 large handfuls of sorrel leaves, or small spinach leaves

2 lemons

4 whole trout, gutted, heads on or off

Freshly milled salt and black pepper

300 ml/½ pint/1¼ cups fish or vegetable stock

2 tbsp sunflower oil

1. Preheat the oven to 200°C, 400°F, Fan 185°C, Gas 6. Butter a wide shallow oven-proof dish large enough for the fish. Finely shred the onions, carrots, courgettes (zucchini) and sorrel leaves. Thinly slice the lemons.

2. Wash the fish, inside and out, and dry with kitchen paper. Season and push the lemon slices into the body cavities.

3. Tip the shredded vegetables into the buttered dish, spread to an even layer and pour over the stock.

4. Lay the fish next to each other on the vegetables, drizzle with a little oil and dot with the butter. Cover with foil, put into the hot oven and cook for 25 minutes, removing the foil for the last 8 minutes for the trout to brown.

Sizzling Venison

No wok? Use a wide shallow frying pan. If stir-fry dishes become too dry as the oil is absorbed, don't add more oil, just add a little hot water.

Serves 4

1 bunch of spring onions (scallions)
350 g/12 oz selection of mini vegetables, such as sweetcorn, pak choi, carrots, courgettes (zucchini), leeks
400 g/14 oz venison frying steak – in large pieces
2 tbsp olive oil
150 ml/¼ pint/⅔ cup venison or beef stock
2 tbsp orange juice
1 tbsp light soy sauce
Handful of beansprouts
Freshly milled black pepper

1. Thinly cut the spring onions (scallions) and mini vegetables to give long strips.

2. Put the venison between two pieces of clear film (plastic wrap) and roll with a rolling pin to a thickness of about 5 mm/¼ inch. Cut into thin strips.

3. Heat a wok or wide deep frying pan, add the oil and cook the vegetables for 2–3 minutes until golden brown. Remove with a slotted spoon. Cook the venison strips over a high heat for a minute until browned. Stir in the stock, orange juice, soy sauce, beansprouts and black pepper. Bring just to the boil, stir in the vegetables and cook for 1–2 minutes. Serve immediately.

Lamb Koftas

Cumin, mint and coriander give minced lamb and
bulgur wheat meatballs lots of flavour.

Serves 4

3 tbsp bulgur wheat

1 small red onion

Large bunch of mint

500 g/1 lb 2 oz lean minced (ground) lamb

2 tsp ground cumin

2 tsp ground coriander

Freshly milled salt and black pepper

Oil, for frying

Dressing

300 ml/½ pint/1¼ cups natural yogurt

½ tsp pepper sauce, optional

Selection of salad leaves, such as rocket, mizuna, frilly lettuce,
  cress and watercress

4 wooden or metal skewers, optional

 Put the kettle on to boil. Tip the bulgur wheat into a bowl and cover with boiling water, leave for 15 minutes, then drain in a sieve and press to remove excess water.

 Finely chop the onion. Pull the mint leaves from the stalks, put half of the small leaves to one side and finely chop the remainder.

 Put the minced (ground) lamb into a bowl and stir in the drained bulgur wheat, onion, cumin, coriander, chopped mint and a little pepper. With a fork, mix together well.

 With wetted hands, divide and shape the mixture into twelve balls.

 Heat the oil in a frying pan and over a medium heat cook the lamb balls, in batches if necessary, for 10–15 minutes, turning occasionally until golden and cooked through.

 Meanwhile prepare the dressing. Tip the yogurt into a bowl and stir in the mint leaves and pepper sauce, if using. Season if necessary.

 Thread the lamb balls onto skewers, if using, serve on a pile of salad leaves and spoon over the dressing.

Belly Pork with Lemon Lentils

*Split red lentils don't need soaking and, unlike some types
of lentils, they do not hold their shape but collapse, which is
perfect for this dish. They absorb all the flavours of the dish
and become like a thick 'gravy'.*

Serves 4

500 g/1 lb 2 oz belly pork

1 onion

1 lemon

6 tomatoes

250 g/9 oz split red lentils

600 ml/1 pint/2½ cups vegetable stock

3 tbsp maple syrup

1 tbsp Worcestershire sauce

Bunch of rocket leaves

Freshly milled salt and black pepper

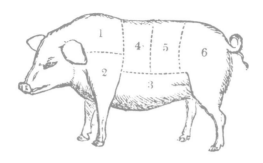

1. ▶ Cut the pork into 5 cm/2 inch pieces. Finely chop the onion. Peel two or three strips of lemon rind, without any pith, cut in half and squeeze the juice. Halve the tomatoes. Rinse and drain the lentils.

2. ▶ Heat a flameproof casserole or heavy-based pan and cook the pork and onion until lightly browned and drain off the fat.

3. ▶ Pour over the stock, bring just to the boil, cover, reduce the heat and cook for 20 minutes.

4. ▶ Stir in the lentils, tomatoes, lemon rind and juice, maple syrup and Worcestershire sauce. Cover and gently cook for a further 25–35 minutes, stirring occasionally (to make sure it doesn't stick) until the pork is cooked through and the lentils are soft. Tear each rocket leaf in half, stir into the pan until wilted.

5. ▶ Season if necessary and serve immediately.

Tarragon Pork with Plums and Tomatoes

A bright and colourful dish with tomatoes of all shapes and colours. Cooking tarragon brings out its anise flavour.

Serves 2

Small bunch of tarragon

½ lemon

4 red plums

1 medium egg

2 bone-in pork chops

55 g/2 oz/¼ cup fresh white breadcrumbs

Freshly milled salt and black pepper

2 tsp olive oil

400 g/14 oz tomatoes, as many colours and varieties
  as you can find

1 ▶ Finely chop the tarragon. Grate the rind from the lemon and squeeze the juice. Halve and stone (pit) the plums. Break the egg into a cup and lightly beat. Cut through the layer of fat at intervals on each pork chop – to prevent them curling.

2 ▶ Put the breadcrumbs into a bowl and stir in the lemon rind and half of the chopped tarragon. Season and stir in enough egg to give a very stiff mixture. With wetted hands, shape the stuffing into 4 balls.

3 ▶ Heat the oil in a large frying pan and fry the chops for 5–6 minutes on each side until browned and cooked through. At the same time cook the stuffing balls until browned and the tomatoes and plums until lightly browned but not totally collapsed. Pour the lemon juice into the pan and scrape up any sediment. Sprinkle over the remaining tarragon and serve immediately.

Ginger Salmon and Beans

*Podded beans or peas can be used in place of the
green beans – just cook for a minute or two longer.*

Serves 2

1 sweet potato
500 g/1 lb 2 oz mixed green beans, such as French beans
  and runner beans
Finger-length piece of fresh root ginger
Two 140 g/5 oz skinless salmon fillets
2 tbsp olive oil
2 tsp sesame seed oil
1 tbsp sesame seeds
1 tsp fish sauce
1 tsp vegetable bouillon powder

1▶ Put the kettle on to boil. Peel the sweet potato and cut into small
cubes. Top and tail the beans and cut into short lengths. Peel the
ginger and cut into matchstick size pieces. Cut the salmon into large
bite-size pieces, removing any bones.

2▶ Put the sweet potato and beans into a large wide shallow pan and
just cover with boiling water (from the kettle). Cook for 5–8
minutes until the beans are tender. Drain and wipe the pan with
kitchen paper. Heat the olive oil and sesame seed oil and cook the
salmon and ginger for 5 minutes until the salmon is golden. Lift
from the pan. Add more oil to the pan if necessary and stir in the
sesame seeds, fish sauce, bouillon powder and 3 tbsp water. Bring to
the boil, return the beans, sweet potato, salmon and ginger to the
pan and, stirring, cook through until piping hot.

Pasta with Purple Sprouting Broccoli and Cashew Nuts

A very simple and fresh pasta dish which isn't spicy. Serve as a meal on its own or as an accompaniment to roasted meats or fish.

Serves 4

2 courgettes (zucchini)
5 tomatoes
140 g/5 oz sugar snap peas
200 g/7 oz purple spouting broccoli spears
Small bunch of sorrel or flat-leaved parsley
500 g/1 lb 2 oz fresh fusilli pasta
3 tbsp olive oil
1 tsp liquid vegetable stock
1 tbsp lemon juice
3 tbsp toasted cashew nuts
Freshly milled salt and black pepper

1. Put the kettle on to boil. Peel the courgettes (zucchini) into long thin strips with a potato peeler. Chop the tomatoes. Cut the sugar snap peas into strips and the broccoli into small pieces. Finely chop the herbs.

2. Cook the pasta according to the packet instructions (using water from the kettle), adding the courgettes (zucchini), sugar snap peas and broccoli for the last 2–3 minutes, until the pasta is cooked and the vegetables are tender.

3. Drain the pasta and vegetables, return to the pan, and stir in the oil to coat. Put the pan over a medium heat and, stirring, add the liquid stock, lemon juice, tomatoes, herbs and nuts. Heat until the tomatoes have just collapsed and the pasta is piping hot. Season to taste and serve immediately.

Apple, Honey, Pumpkin and Sunflower Seed Cake

This spicy, seed-topped, wholemeal cake hides layers of apple. Eat as a cake or dessert. Serve with scoops of vanilla ice cream, crème fraîche or piping hot custard.

Serves 4

115 g/4 oz/½ cup butter plus extra for greasing

4 medium cooking apples

200 g/7 oz/1¾ cups white self-raising flour

60 g/2¼ oz/8 tbsp wholemeal self-raising flour

2 tsp ground mixed spice

115 g/4 oz/½ cup muscovado brown sugar

2 medium eggs

A little milk, if needed

1 tbsp pumpkin seeds

1 tbsp sunflower seeds

3 tbsp clear honey

1. Preheat the oven to 200°C, 400°F, Fan 185°C, Gas 6. Butter a shallow oven-proof dish measuring about 25 x 17.5 cm/10 x 7 inches.

2. Quarter the apples, remove the cores and thinly slice.

3. Sift the two types of flour and mixed spice into a mixing bowl and stir in any bits of grain left in the sieve. Cut the butter into small pieces and add to the flour mixture. Using your fingertips, rub the butter into the flour until the mixture resembles fine crumbs (or do this part in a food processor). Stir in the sugar, eggs and enough milk to give a soft sticky mix.

4. Roughly spread a third of the mixture in the dish and cover with half of the apple pieces. Repeat with a third of the mix and the remaining apple. Spread over the remaining cake mix. Leave the surface quite rough. Scatter over the pumpkin and sunflower seeds and drizzle over the honey.

5. Put into the hot oven and cook for 30–40 minutes until the top is crisp and golden.

Pancake Toasties with Prawns (Shrimps) and Mozzarella

Like a toasted sandwich but with pancakes in place of the bread. Serve as a snack or with salad leaves and coleslaw for a light meal. Replace the prawns (shrimps) with smoked or spicy ham.

Serves 2

70 g/2½ oz mozzarella cheese

2 tomatoes

200 g/7 oz cooked, peeled prawns (shrimps)

4 ready-prepared pancakes

2 tbsp onion relish

8 basil leaves

8 spinach leaves

Freshly milled black pepper

Butter, for cooking

Sunflower oil, for cooking

▶ Slice or tear the mozzarella into small pieces. Cut the tomatoes into thin slices and chop the prawns (shrimps).

▶ Spread the centre of each pancake with a little onion relish and cover with the basil and spinach leaves. Put the tomato slices, mozzarella and prawns (shrimps) on top and season with a little pepper. Fold the sides over the filling to give a parcel shape.

▶ Heat the butter and oil in a wide frying pan and fry the pancakes for 2–3 minutes each side until crisp and golden. Serve immediately.

Hot Creamy Rhubarb Fool with Maple Syrup

Rhubarb and custard is a dream combination and peanut brittle adds crunch. Serve with thin crisp biscuits and edible flowers.

Serves 4

1 lime
400 g/14 oz rhubarb
100 g/3½ oz peanut brittle
150 ml/¼ pint/⅔ cup unsweetened apple juice
3 tbsp maple syrup
¼ tsp ground mixed spice
115 g/4 oz/½ cup caster sugar
300 ml/½ pint/1¼ cups ready-made custard
150 ml/¼ pint/⅔ cup double (heavy) cream

1. Finely grate the rind from the lime, cut in half and squeeze the juice. Cut the rhubarb into bite-sized pieces. Break the peanut brittle into small pieces, put into a freezer bag and tap with the end of a rolling pin until in small pieces.

2. Pour the apple juice into a flame-proof dish which can go from hob to table (or use a medium saucepan). Stir in the maple syrup, spice, sugar, lime rind and juice, then heat until almost boiling. Reduce the heat, add the rhubarb and cook for 8–12 minutes until soft but not mushy.

3. Reduce the heat and carefully stir in the custard and cream. Scatter the peanut brittle over the top and serve immediately.

4. To serve cold, omit the peanut brittle, chill the dessert and add the peanut brittle when it's served.

Lemon and Lime Baked Cheesecake

*In spring we eagerly wait the first fruits to appear,
but don't forget lemons and limes. Delicious and
refreshing, this cheesecake will fill a gap.*

Serves 6

½ small lemon

1 small lime

375 g/13 oz packet ready-rolled shortcrust pastry

250 g/9 oz curd cheese

55 g/2 oz/¼ cup soft brown sugar

150 ml/¼ pint/⅔ cup soured cream

3 medium eggs, separated

3 tbsp apricot conserve

Icing sugar, to sift

▶ Preheat the oven to 200°C, 400°F, Fan 185°C, Gas 6. Finely grate the rinds from the lemon and lime, cut the lime in half, squeezing the juice from one half.

▶ Unroll the pastry and use to line a deep 23 cm/9 inch flan ring, trim any excess pastry. Scrunch some foil and put into the pastry case. Put into the hot oven and bake 'blind' for 10 minutes.

▶ Remove and lift out the foil. Reduce the oven temperature to 180°C, 350°F, Fan 165°C, Gas 4.

▶ In one bowl mix together the curd cheese, sugar, lemon and lime rinds, lime juice, soured cream and egg yolks. In a separate bowl stiffly whisk the egg whites and carefully fold into the curd cheese mixture.

▶ Spread the conserve over the base of the flan case and spoon over the filling.

▶ Put into the hot oven and cook for 40–45 minutes until firm and golden. Leave in the tin a few minutes before removing. Sift a little icing sugar on top and serve hot or cold.

Oat and Almond Rhubarb Crumble

*Juicy young pale pink stems of rhubarb with a nutty sweet topping.
Serve with thick yogurt, crème fraîche or vanilla ice-cream.*

Serves 4

500 g/1 lb 2 oz rhubarb
150 ml/¼ pint/⅔ cup orange juice
4 tbsp clear honey
1 tsp cornflour (cornstarch)

Topping
70 g/2½ oz/9 tbsp plain wholemeal (whole-wheat) flour
100 g/3½ oz flaked oats (porridge oats)
85 g/3 oz/6 tbsp unsalted butter
115 g/4 oz/½ cup light brown sugar
2 tbsp ground almonds

1. Preheat the oven to 180°C, 350°F, Fan 165°C, Gas 4. Cut the rhubarb stalks into bite-sized pieces. Pour the orange juice into a small bowl and stir in the honey and cornflour (cornstarch).

2. Tip the fruit in a shallow oven-proof dish about 850 ml/1½ pint/3½ cup capacity. Pour over the blended cornflour (cornstarch) mixture.

3. For the topping, tip the flour and oats into a bowl. Cut the butter into small pieces and add to the flour/oat mixture. Using your fingertips, rub the butter into the mix until it resembles coarse crumbs. Stir in the sugar and almonds.

4. Sprinkle the topping thickly and evenly over the fruit, pressing down lightly.

5. Put into the hot oven and bake for 30–40 minutes until cooked and golden.

Summer

AH, THOSE lazy, balmy, glorious summer days – at least that's what you hope for until you get there and see what climate change has done to our weather.

But whether it's a sizzling summer or a damp squib, you can be sure of a plentiful supply of vegetables – aubergines (eggplants), asparagus, summer squash with thin edible skins, courgettes (zucchini), tomatoes and mange-touts – to go with shellfish, poussin, noodles, rice, salmon or mackerel – and, yes, with barbecue flavours for those al fresco opportunities. Just sample Clams and Spaghetti with Shredded Vegetables (page 70), Tuna with Fennel, Tomatoes and Rocket (page 72) and Poussin and Roasted Vegetables with Fresh Plum Salsa (page 78).

Summer herbs are so exciting. I like to take full advantage of their bright colours and lively flavours by using half of the allotted quantity in the cooking, with the other half reserved for shredding and throwing into the pan right at the end – see for example Broad Beans, Runner Beans, Peas and Mange-Touts (page 67) – so half cooked and half almost raw for maximum effect.

And summer wouldn't be summer without luscious ripe fruits, like cherries, grapes, peaches, strawberries and gooseberries – try them in four delicious desserts.

Chilled Green Pea and Watercress Soup

Fabulous green colour, chilled soups are very refreshing on hot summer days. Pea shoots are the tendrils and small leaves at the top of the plants and have an intense pea taste. Look for them in markets or stores. Serve with a swirl of yogurt or soured cream.

Serves 4–6

2 shallots

1 little gem lettuce

1 bunch of watercress

25 g/1 oz/2 tbsp butter

1 vegetable stock cube

200 g/7 oz peas – no need to thaw if frozen

2 sprigs of mint

1 star anise

Freshly milled salt and black pepper

Handful of pea shoots, optional

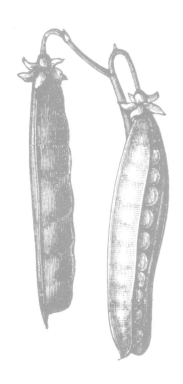

1. Put the kettle on to boil. Finely chop the shallots. Pull the lettuce apart and remove the leaves from the watercress.

2. Melt the butter in a medium saucepan and cook gently for about 5 minutes, stirring occasionally, until beginning to soften but not brown. Pour in 1 litre/1¾ pints/4¼ cups boiling water (from the kettle) and add the stock cube, shallots, peas, mint and star anise. Bring just to the boil, reduce the heat and cook gently for 10 minutes. Stir in the lettuce and watercress and cook for a further 5 minutes or until the peas are cooked.

3. Remove the star anise and, using a stick blender, whiz until fairly smooth and season if necessary. Serve hot or cold with the pea shoots on top, if using.

Oriental Prawn (Shrimp) Soup with Leaves

Radishes may seem an odd inclusion in this soup but they add a peppery taste and some heat.

Serves 4–6

6 spring onions (scallions)
Small piece of ginger
6 radishes
1 lemon grass stalk
Large handful of pak choi leaves or Chinese leaves
1.2 litres/2 pints/5 cups chicken stock
2 tsp light soy sauce
2 tsp sesame oil
250 g/9 oz cooked shelled large prawns (shrimps), thawed if frozen

Thinly slice the spring onions (scallions) and grate the ginger. Trim the radishes, leaving a few leaves attached, and slice in half from leaf to root. Bruise the lemon grass a little by tapping with the back of a knife. Finely slice the pak choi or Chinese leaves.

Pour the stock into a large pan and add the spring onions (scallions), ginger, radishes, lemon grass, soy sauce and sesame oil. Bring just to the boil, reduce the heat and cook gently for 8 minutes. Stir in the prawns (shrimps) and leaves and cook for a further 3–5 minutes until the leaves have wilted and the prawns (shrimps) are piping hot.

Remove the lemon grass before serving.

Corn-on-the-Cob with Sticky Nutty Sesame Glaze

Buy fresh cobs which are heavy for their size and peel away the leaves and silky strands. Don't add salt when cooking the corn initially as it will toughen the kernels. Serve with bread to mop up the juices and napkins to catch the drips.

Serves 2

2 cobs of sweet corn

Small handful of unsalted peanuts

3 tbsp butter

2 tbsp clear honey

1 tbsp sesame seeds

1. Cut each cob of sweet corn into three or four, depending on size. Chop the peanuts, not too fine.

2. Put the cobs in a medium saucepan of water, cover, bring to the boil and cook for 10 minutes or until the kernels are tender and would easily come away from the cob, then drain and dry on kitchen paper.

3. Wipe the pan dry with kitchen paper, return to the hob and stir in the butter, honey, peanuts and sesame seeds. Heat until the mixture just starts to bubble.

4. With a slotted spoon or tongs put the cobs into the pan. Turning them frequently, cook until golden. Be careful not to let the sauce burn.

Spiced Jerk Pork Salad

Jerk is a hot spicy seasoning blend which originated in Jamaica. The hot, spiced pork and juices cause the salad leaves to wilt. An easy recipe to multiply to serve more. Serve with hot crusty baguettes and mayonnaise on the side.

Serves 2

2 boneless pork chops

1 red chilli (see page 13)

Large bunch of chives

1 sprig of fresh thyme

2 tsp brown sugar

½ tsp ground cinnamon

½ tsp ground ginger

½ tsp ground allspice

Pinch of ground cloves

2 tbsp sunflower oil

3 tbsp unsweetened pineapple juice

Mixed salad leaves

1. ▶ Trim any fat from the chops and cut into narrow strips. Halve the chilli, remove and discard the seeds and finely chop. Thinly slice the chives. Pull the leaves from the sprig of thyme.

2. ▶ Put the sugar in a food (freezer) bag and add the thyme leaves, cinnamon, ginger, allspice and cloves. Add the pieces of pork and shake until thoroughly coated. If there's time chill the seasoned meat for 1–2 hours for the flavours to develop.

3. ▶ Heat a frying pan until hot, add the oil and chilli and cook the pork until golden and cooked through. Lift from the pan and keep warm.

4. ▶ Add the pineapple juice and chives to the hot pan and bubble for 1 minute until slightly thickened, stirring in any crusty sediment from around the edges of the pan. Pile the salad leaves on plates, scatter the pork over and drizzle the pan juices over the top. Eat straight away.

Hot Steak Sandwich with Creamy Beetroot (Beet) Salad

An up-market sandwich for carnivores. Wear disposable gloves when handling beetroots (beets) as they stain. It is also delicious in flour tortillas or sourdough bread.

Serves 2

2 fillet or sirloin beef steaks

1 tbsp Dijon mustard

1 tbsp Worcestershire sauce

2 tbsp olive oil

Freshly milled salt and black pepper

3 small raw beetroots (beets), weighing about 200 g/7 oz

150 ml/¼ pint/⅔ cup soured cream

1 tbsp orange juice

5 spring onions (scallions)

4 gherkins

2 large baguettes, warmed

Large handful of salad leaves

1. Trim the steaks and pat dry with kitchen paper. In a small bowl mix together the Dijon mustard, Worcestershire sauce, 1 tbsp of the oil and a little pepper. Spread over both sides of the steaks and leave to marinade for 1–2 hours if possible.

2. Scrub the beetroots (beets) and coarsely grate. Put into a bowl and stir in the soured cream and orange juice. Thinly slice the spring onions (scallions) and roughly chop the gherkins. Add to the beetroot (beet) salad and season if necessary.

3. Heat the remaining oil in a griddle or frying pan until very hot, add the steaks and cook for 2 minutes a side for rare or longer if you prefer. Cut each steak into strips.

4. Slice open the baguettes and fill with salad leaves, the beetroot (beet) salad and top with the hot steak.

Minted New Potatoes with Lemon Balm

Lemon and mint are a good combination of flavours with potatoes. Serve hot or cold with salads, meats or fish.

Serves 4

900 g/2 lb small new potatoes
Small bunch of mint
Small bunch of lemon balm
1 bunch of spring onions (scallions)
100 g/3½ oz pine nuts
2 tsp vegetable bouillon powder
2 tbsp olive oil
Freshly milled salt and black pepper

1▷ Put the kettle on to boil. Scrub the potatoes to remove the skins, or leave the skins on. Pull the leaves off half the sprigs of mint and all the sprigs of lemon balm. Thinly slice the spring onions (scallions). Finely chop the pine nuts.

2▷ Put the potatoes into a saucepan, pour over sufficient boiling water (from the kettle) to just cover the potatoes, stir in the bouillon powder and the remaining sprigs of mint. Cover and cook for 12–15 minutes, or until just tender.

3▷ Drain the potatoes, discard the mint and put the potatoes back into the hot pan. Pour over the oil and stir in the spring onions (scallions) and pine nuts. Stirring, cook for 2–3 minutes until the oil sizzles. Remove from the heat, stir in the mint leaves and lemon balm leaves and season if necessary.

4▷ Serve immediately whilst piping hot, or to serve cold, cover and chill.

Broad Beans, Runner Beans, Peas and Mange-Touts

Summer vegetables in a creamy sauce. Crème fraîche is very useful because it doesn't curdle when boiled. If you are using peas or broad beans in their pods just double the weight given.

Serves 4 as an accompaniment or 2 as a light meal

200 g/7 oz runner beans
200 g/7 oz mange-touts
Small bunch of dill or chervil
200 g/7 oz shelled peas
200 g/7 oz shelled broad beans
2 tsp vegetable bouillon powder
300 ml/½ pint/1¼ cups crème fraîche
Freshly milled salt and black pepper

Put the kettle on to boil. Top and tail the runner beans, removing any stringy pieces, and slice horizontally into long thin strips. Trim the mange-touts and slice each diagonally into three. Chop the dill or chervil.

Put the peas, broad beans and runner beans into a saucepan, pour over sufficient water (from the kettle) to just cover, stir in the bouillon powder, cover and cook for 8 minutes. Add the mange-touts and cook for 3–4 minutes until the vegetables are tender.

Drain the vegetables and put back into the hot pan. Stir in the crème fraîche and half of the chopped herbs. Stirring bring just to the boil, season if necessary, stir in the remaining herbs and serve immediately.

Aubergines with Rice and Pepper Filling

*You can serve these hot or cold – in hotter climates
stuffed aubergines (eggplants) are left to cool then
drizzled with olive oil and eaten as part of a mezze.*

Serves 2

1 small yellow pepper
3 yellow tomatoes
2 spring onions (scallions)
Small bunch of coriander
2 aubergines (eggplants)
2 tbsp lemon juice
2 tsp olive oil, plus extra for brushing
3 tbsp ready-cooked brown rice
1 tsp ground paprika pepper
1 tsp ground cumin

 Put the kettle on to boil. Preheat the oven to 180°C, 350°F, Fan 165°C, Gas 4. Cut the pepper in half, remove and discard the seeds and finely chop. Roughly chop the tomatoes and thinly slice the spring onions (scallions). Finely chop the coriander.

 Cut the aubergines (eggplants) in half lengthways. With a spoon scoop out some of the flesh from each half to leave a hollow shell. Brush the insides with a little lemon juice to prevent browning and brush the outsides with a little oil. Arrange them in a wide shallow ovenproof dish.

 Finely chop the scooped-out aubergine (eggplant) flesh and put into a bowl. Stir in the pepper, tomatoes, spring onions (scallions), coriander, rice, paprika and cumin. Mix in any remaining lemon juice and oil.

 Spoon the filling into the aubergine (eggplant) shells and pour a little hot water (from the kettle) in the bottom of the dish to a depth of about 2 cm/¾ inch.

 Cover, put into the hot oven and cook for 35–45 minutes until the vegetables are tender.

Clams and Spaghetti with Shredded Vegetables

No clams in their shells? Then use mussels or a bag of mixed seafood. Serve with a glass of chilled white wine and crusty bread.

Serves 4–6

800 g/1 lb 12 oz clams in their shells
2 courgettes (zucchini)
2 carrots
5 spring onions (scallions)
1 bunch of dill
1 lemon
350 g/12 oz spaghetti
2 tbsp olive oil
150 ml/¼ pint/⅔ cup fish or vegetable stock
150 ml/¼ pint/⅔ cup dry vermouth
2 tbsp capers
Freshly milled black pepper

1. Scrub the clams, discarding any with broken shells and any that do not close when given a sharp knock. Cut the courgettes (zucchini), carrots and spring onions (scallions) into long thin strips. Finely chop the dill. Grate the rind from the lemon, cut in half and squeeze the juice.

2. Cook the spaghetti according to the packet instructions until just cooked, but 5 minutes before the end of the cooking time add the shredded vegetables to the pan, bring back to the boil and cook for 2 minutes.

3. Remove from the heat, drain and quickly stir in the lemon rind and juice, oil, stock, vermouth and clams. Return to the heat and cook over a gentle heat, stirring until the clams have just opened (discard any that haven't). Stir in the dill and capers and season with a little black pepper.

4. Serve immediately.

71

Tuna with Fennel, Tomatoes and Rocket

Tuna is a very elegant fish with no waste and cooks perfectly in the microwave. It is cooked 'pink', but just cook for a few seconds longer if you prefer it cooked through.

Serves 2

1 shallot
1 medium fennel bulb
3 medium red tomatoes
3 medium yellow tomatoes
Large handful of rocket leaves
Small bunch of fresh fennel leaves
150 ml/¼ pint/⅔ cup fish or vegetable stock
Freshly milled black pepper
2 fresh tuna steaks

1. Finely chop the shallot and fennel bulb. Roughly chop the red and yellow tomatoes. Tear the rocket leaves if very large. Finely chop the fennel leaves.

2. Pour the stock into a wide microwave-proof casserole and mix in the shallot, fennel bulb, tomatoes, half the fennel leaves and a little pepper. Cover and cook on High for 5 minutes until the shallot and fennel has softened.

3. Stir in the rocket leaves and put the tuna steaks on top. Sprinkle the remaining fennel leaves over the fish.

4. Cover and cook on High for 2 minutes until the fish is cooked on the outside but still pink inside (or ½–1 minute longer if you prefer it cooked all the way through).

5. Spoon the vegetables onto plates and top with the tuna steaks.

Mackerel Fillets with Gooseberries and Bulgur Wheat

Rich oily mackerel is offset by sharp tangy gooseberries.

Serves 4

350 g/12 oz bulgur wheat
1 small onion
1 garlic clove
200 g/7 oz gooseberries
1 small lime
Small bunch of fresh coriander
3 tbsp olive oil
2 tbsp liquid vegetable stock
8 mackerel fillets
Freshly milled salt and black pepper

1. Put the kettle on to boil. Preheat the oven to 200°C, 400°F, Fan 185°C, Gas 6. Tip the bulgur wheat into a large bowl, pour over boiling water (from the kettle) to cover, stir and leave to soak for 20–30 minutes, then drain through a fine sieve.

2. Finely chop the onion and crush the garlic. Top and tail the gooseberries and cut in half. Grate the rind from the lime, cut in half and squeeze the juice. Finely chop the coriander.

3. Heat 1 tbsp of oil in a wide flameproof shallow dish and cook the onion and garlic for 5 minutes until softened but not browned. Remove from the heat and stir in the rind and juice of the lime, the gooseberries, drained bulgur wheat, coriander, 1 tbsp of oil, vegetable stock and 150ml/¼ pint/⅔ cup boiling water. Stir well, cover and put into the hot oven for 10 minutes.

4. Remove from the oven, uncover, and arrange the mackerel fillets on top, brushed with a little oil. Return to the hot oven and cook for a further 10–12 minutes until the fish is cooked through. Season if necessary and serve immediately.

Crab and Noodles with Chilli and Ginger Coconut Broth

Not as liquid as a soup, but a light brothy summer 'stew', a very refreshing dish without added oil.

Serves 4–6

300 g/10½ oz rice noodles

1 small leek

5 tomatoes

100 g/3½ oz thin green beans

1 small red pepper

1 red chilli (see page 13)

Small bunch of coriander leaves

About 3 cm/1¼ inch piece of fresh root ginger

350 g/12 oz cooked crabmeat

400 ml/14 fl oz/1⅔ cups chicken stock

150 ml/¼ pint/⅔ cup coconut milk

1 tbsp lime juice

Freshly milled salt and black pepper

1. Put the kettle on to boil. Put the noodles into a large bowl, cover with boiling water (from the kettle) and leave to soak.

2. Very finely shred the leek. Roughly chop the tomatoes and cut each bean into three. Halve the red pepper, remove and discard the seeds and stalk and cut into thin slices. Cut the chilli in half, remove and discard the seeds and thinly slice. Finely chop the coriander and grate the ginger.

3. Cut the crabmeat into bite-size pieces.

4. Pour the stock and coconut milk into a large saucepan and stir in the leek, tomatoes, beans, red pepper, chilli, ginger, and lime juice. Bring to the boil and cook for 4–5 minutes until the vegetables have softened.

5. Drain the noodles, add to the pan and cook for 2–3 minutes until piping hot. Stir in the crabmeat and coriander and cook for a further 2 minutes. Season if necessary and serve immediately.

Salmon Fillets with Capers and Tarragon

A speedy dish cooked in the microwave, tarragon has a wonderful flavour when cooked – very aromatic with an anise-like flavour. Serve with marsh samphire, if you come across it in the fishmongers – also called sea asparagus, it is found on the seashore. It has a short season, mid to late summer and slightly beyond, depending on where you live. It becomes woody towards the end of the season. Cook in boiling water for a few minutes until tender.

Serves 2

1 large orange

Large handful of spinach leaves

6 cherry-sized plum tomatoes

Large bunch of tarragon

2 tbsp capers

150 ml/¼ pint/⅔ cup fish or vegetable stock

Two 175 g/6 oz skinless salmon fillets

25 g/1 oz/2 tbsp butter

Freshly milled salt and black pepper

1. Finely grate the rind from half of the orange, peel the orange, remove the segments and cut in half. Finely shred the spinach leaves. Quarter the tomatoes and remove the tarragon leaves from the stalks. Rinse the capers to remove any excess brine.

2. Pour the stock into a large microwave-proof casserole and stir in the orange rind. Mix in the spinach, tomatoes, orange pieces and capers. Cover and cook on High, stirring once, for 2 minutes until softened.

3. Stir in half of the tarragon leaves, put the fish fillets on top, spaced apart, dot with small pieces of butter and sprinkle over the remaining leaves.

4. Cover and cook on High for 3 minutes or until the salmon is just cooked. Season if necessary and serve immediately.

Poussin and Roasted Vegetables with Fresh Plum Salsa

Poussins are young chickens. Orange slices and sprigs of rosemary in the body cavity of the poussins are a simple way of giving lots of extra flavour to the roasted birds.

Serves 2

4 sprigs of rosemary

2 oranges

2 small whole garlic bulbs

1 red onion

2 small fennel bulbs

2 sweet potatoes

2 courgettes (zucchini)

Freshly milled salt and black pepper

2 tsp olive oil

2 poussins

Salsa

250 g/9 oz plums

1 shallot

A small piece of fresh root ginger

2 tbsp clear honey

3 tbsp orange juice

1. Preheat the oven to 200°C, 400°F, Fan 185°C, Gas 6. Heat a large roasting tin. Pull the leaves from the rosemary sprigs and roughly chop. Halve and thinly slice the oranges. Slice the tops off each garlic bulb. Quarter the onion and fennel bulbs and slice the sweet potatoes into wedges. Cut the courgettes (zucchini) into three or four large pieces depending on their size.

2. Put the vegetables and garlic into a large bowl and stir in half the rosemary, seasoning and 1 tbsp of the oil.

3. Remove any ties from the poussins and with a sharp knife or scissors trim the ends of the legs, if necessary. Lightly season inside and out, push the orange slices and a little rosemary into the body cavities. Rub with oil and sprinkle over more rosemary.

4. Lift the poussins into the hot roasting tin and scatter the vegetables around in a single layer. Put into the hot oven and cook for 45–55 minutes until golden brown and cooked through. (To check, insert a skewer into the thickest part of the thigh – the juices should run clear.)

5. Meanwhile prepare the salsa – cut the plums in half, remove the stones (pits) and finely chop. Grate the shallot and ginger. Mix the honey and orange juice in a bowl and stir in the chopped plums, shallot and ginger, season if necessary. Chill until needed.

Picnic Frittata

A deep savoury omelette, perfect for cutting into wedges and eating out of doors. For a drinks do, serve in small wedges speared onto cocktail sticks. There seem to be a lot of ingredients for an omelette, but what flavours.

Serves 4–6

6 small new potatoes
6 spring onions (scallions)
1 red pepper
1 courgette (zucchini)
2 garlic cloves
Small handful of parsley
Small handful of mint
100 g/3½ oz Cheddar cheese
9 large eggs
150 ml/¼ pint/⅔ cup single cream
Freshly milled salt and black pepper
100 g/3½ oz fresh peas
25 g/1 oz/2 tbsp butter
3 tbsp olive oil

1. Put the kettle on to boil. Peel, halve and thinly slice the potatoes. Thinly slice the spring onions (scallions). Halve the pepper, remove and discard the seeds and stalk and cut into small pieces. Grate the courgette (zucchini), crush the garlic and finely chop the parsley and mint. Finely grate the cheese.

2. Break the eggs into a bowl, stir in 2 tbsp cold water, the cream, cheese, garlic, parsley, mint and seasoning.

3. Arrange the potatoes and peas over the base of a large non-stick frying pan and cover with boiling water (from the kettle). Cook for 3–5 minutes until cooked, then drain. Clean the pan and reheat it. Add the butter and 2 tbsp of oil. Stir in the spring onions (scallions), red pepper, courgette (zucchini), and cook on a medium heat for 5 minutes until softened.

4. Return the potatoes and peas to the pan and pour the egg mixture over. Cook on a low heat until the egg mixture has begun to set, do not stir.

5. Carefully invert the omelette onto a large plate. Add the remaining oil to the pan and carefully slide the omelette into the pan, cooked side uppermost. Cook gently until browned on the other side, alternatively brown the top under a hot grill (broiler).

6. Cut into wedges and eat hot or cold.

Rosemary Lamb Steaks with Roasted Peppers and Tomatoes

Lamb leg steaks on the bone are a particularly tasty cut of meat and they act like saucers to hold the topping mix of orange, rosemary and breadcrumbs.

Serves 2

2 small red (bell) peppers

3 rosemary sprigs

2 lamb leg steaks, about 175 g/6 oz, on the bone

2 tbsp olive oil

Freshly milled salt and black pepper

4 tbsp fresh breadcrumbs

2 tbsp orange juice

8–10 small new potatoes, skins on

2 tbsp redcurrant jelly

2 sprays of tomatoes on the vine (each with 3–4 tomatoes)

1. ▶ Put the kettle on to boil. Preheat the oven to 200°C, 400°F, Fan 185°C, Gas 6. Cut the (bell) peppers in half, remove the stalks and scoop out the seeds. Pull the leaves from the rosemary and finely chop. Brush the steaks with a little of the oil and season with pepper.

2. ▶ For the topping, put the breadcrumbs into a small bowl and stir in the orange juice, 2 tsp of the chopped rosemary and a little seasoning.

3. ▶ Put the potatoes into a bowl and stir in the oil, the rest of the rosemary and a little seasoning.

4. ▶ Put the steaks into a shallow roasting tin and spoon the potatoes around the edge. (Reserve the oil and rosemary mix.) Put into the hot oven and cook for 15 minutes.

5. ▶ Carefully turn the (bell) pepper halves and sprays of tomatoes in the oil and rosemary mix.

6. ▶ Turn the potatoes and the steaks. Spoon half of the topping onto each steak, pressing down with the back of a spoon and add the (bell) peppers to the tin. Cook for 15 minutes.

7. ▶ Put the redcurrant jelly into a small bowl and stir in 3 tbsp boiling water (from the kettle), pour over the (bell) peppers to glaze and put the tomatoes (still on the vines) in the tin and cook for 5–8 minutes until the steaks are cooked through and the vegetables roasted.

8. ▶ Serve the steaks and vegetables with the juices spooned over.

Ratatouille with Chickpeas

A seasonal mix of tomatoes, (bell) peppers, courgettes (zucchini) and herbs, simmered until softened. I like lots of garlic in this dish, but just use less if preferred. Works well with most cooked beans or lentils. Serve hot or cold with crusty bread to mop up the juices.

Serves 4

2 red onions
500 g/1 lb 2 oz tomatoes
2 red (bell) peppers
2 orange (bell) peppers
4 courgettes (zucchini)
4 garlic cloves, optional
Small handful of parsley leaves
Large handful of basil leaves
400 g/14 oz can chickpeas or flageolet beans
2 tbsp olive oil
300 ml/½ pint/1¼ cups vegetable stock
½ tsp sugar
Freshly milled salt and black pepper

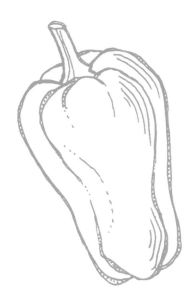

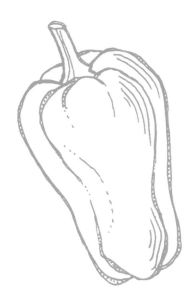 Thinly slice the onions. Roughly chop the tomatoes. Halve the red and orange (bell) peppers, remove and discard the seeds and stalk and cut into small pieces. Thinly slice the courgettes (zucchini) and crush the garlic. Finely chop the parsley and tear the basil leaves, if large. Drain and rinse the chickpeas or beans.

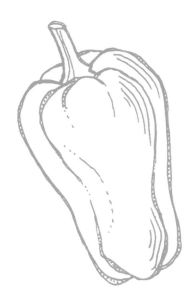 Heat the oil in a saucepan and stir in the onions, tomatoes, (bell) peppers, courgettes (zucchini) and garlic. Cook over a medium heat for 10 minutes until beginning to soften and brown, stirring.

 Pour over the stock and stir in the chickpeas or beans, sugar, a little seasoning, and half of the parsley and basil. Bring just to the boil, then cover and cook very gently for 15–20 minutes, stirring occasionally until the vegetables are soft, adding a little more stock if the mixture becomes too dry. Stir in the remaining parsley and basil.

Baba Ghanoush

A Middle-Eastern purée of aubergine (eggplant) and tahini — sesame seed paste. One of my favourite dips or spreads and so delicious you'll probably want to make a larger quantity. Serve with hot flat breads to spread and with salad ingredients to dunk and scoop.

Serves 2–4

Juice of 2 lemons
2 garlic cloves
Small bunch of mint
2 medium aubergines (eggplants)
3 tbsp olive oil
6 tbsp tahini (sesame seed paste)
Freshly milled salt and white pepper
2 tbsp pomegranate seeds, optional

1. Slice the lemons in half and squeeze the juice. Slice the garlic. Pull the mint leaves from the stalks, select a few small ones to leave whole and finely chop the remainder.

2. Cut the aubergines (eggplants) lengthways into three slices and brush with a little of the oil.

3. Heat a heavy-based griddle pan and cook the aubergine (eggplant) slices (in batches if necessary) until golden and soft, turning once. Leave to cool.

4. Scoop the flesh from the skins and using a stick-blender process the aubergine (eggplant), tahini and garlic until smooth. Spoon into a bowl and stir in the olive oil, lemon juice and chopped mint. Season to taste.

5. Scatter the mint leaves and pomegranate seeds, if using, over the top.

Summer Chicken with Coloured Rice

Rather like a colourful risotto or pilaf, a whole meal in a pan. Different types of rice can have slightly different cooking times so some will be soft and some have a bite.

Serves 4

2 leeks
300 g/10½ oz tomatoes
140 g/5 oz summer cabbage
1 bunch of watercress
300 g/10½ oz mixed rice, such as Red Camargue, brown rice,
  Jasmine rice and wild rice which is a grass
450 g/1 lb boneless chicken
2 tbsp olive oil
600 ml/1 pint/2½ cups chicken stock
Freshly milled salt and black pepper

Thinly slice the leeks. Roughly chop the tomatoes and finely shred the cabbage. Pull the leaves from the watercress stalks and thinly slice the stalks. Rinse the rice under running water. Cut the chicken into large bite-size pieces.

Heat the oil in a heavy-based saucepan and cook the chicken until browned. Stir in the leeks, watercress stalks, tomatoes, stock and rice. Bring just to the boil, reduce the heat, cover and cook for 20 minutes.

Stir in the cabbage and cook for a further 15 minutes until the chicken is cooked through and the rice is tender. Stir in the watercress leaves and season to taste. Serve immediately.

Spiced Chicken and Summer Squash with Cucumber Dressing

Honey and spices give a spicy sticky coating to chicken and squash. Serve with a crisp salad of summer leaves and hot garlic bread.

Serves 4

700 g/1 lb 9 oz summer squash
2 tbsp olive oil
2 tsp sesame seed oil
2 tbsp clear honey
2 tbsp smooth mango chutney
1 tbsp tomato purée
½ tsp five spice powder
2 tbsp sesame seeds
Freshly milled salt and pepper
12 chicken drumsticks

Dressing
1 cucumber
6 spring onions (scallions)
400 ml/14 fl oz thick Greek natural yogurt

1. Preheat the oven to 200°C, 400°F, Fan 185°C, Gas 6. Peel the thick skin from the squash and cut into wedges or large pieces.

2. Pour the olive and sesame seed oils into a large bowl, then stir in the honey, chutney, tomato purée, five spice powder, sesame seeds and a little seasoning if wished. Add the chicken and squash and turn until well coated.

3. Spread them in a single layer in a roasting tin and put into the hot oven. Cook for 30 minutes, turning them both once until the squash is golden and the chicken is cooked through – juices should run clear when pierced with a skewer or sharp knife.

4. Meanwhile, prepare the dressing. Cut the cucumber in half lengthways. Scoop out the seeds and coarsely grate. Finely slice the spring onions (scallions). Spoon the yogurt into a bowl and add the cucumber and spring onions (scallions). Mix well and season to taste.

Noodles with Spiced Mustard Kidneys and Bacon

The fresh tomato and pepper sauce is flavoured with parsley and thyme as well as wholegrain mustard.

Serves 2

200 g/7 oz thick rice noodles

1 small onion

4 tomatoes

1 small red (bell) pepper

Small bunch of parsley

Sprig of fresh thyme

2 lean back bacon rashers (strips)

6 lambs' kidneys

1 tbsp plain (all-purpose) flour

Freshly milled salt and black pepper

1 tbsp sunflower oil

300 ml/½ pint/1¼ cups vegetable stock

1 tbsp wholegrain mustard

1. Put the noodles into a large bowl and cover with cold water and leave to soak. Thinly slice the onion. Roughly chop the tomatoes. Halve the red (bell) pepper, remove and discard the seeds and stalk and cut into thin slices. Finely chop the parsley and pull the small thyme leaves from the woody stalks. Trim the rinds from the bacon and cut into thin strips.

2. Wash the kidneys, halve, and with scissors remove the cores. Cut into slices. Put the flour in a food (freezer) bag, add a little seasoning and the slices of kidney. Shake until thoroughly coated.

3. Heat the oil in a saucepan and cook the onion for 5 minutes until softened but not browned. Stir in the coated kidney slices and bacon strips and cook until browned all over, stirring to prevent sticking.

4. Pour over the stock and add the tomatoes, red (bell) pepper, thyme leaves, half the parsley and mustard. Bring just to the boil, reduce the heat, cover and cook for 15 minutes until the kidneys are cooked.

5. Drain the noodles and add to the pan with the remaining parsley. Cook for 3–5 minutes until the noodles are piping hot.

Smoked Salmon and Asparagus Pasta

Smoked salmon is as delicious hot as cold. The creamy sauce just coats the pasta and looks a sophisticated dish. Pasta comes in endless shapes, use your favourite. Dramatic if you use squid ink pasta which is black.

Serves 4

200 g/7 oz smoked salmon
280 g/10 oz asparagus spears
350 g/12 oz spinach or tomato flavoured pasta – your choice of shape
1 tbsp olive oil
150 ml/¼ pint/⅔ cup vegetable stock
150 ml/¼ pint/⅔ cup double (heavy) cream
3 tbsp grated Parmesan cheese
Freshly milled black pepper

1. Cut the salmon into strips, about 2 cm/¾ inch wide. Trim the woody end of the asparagus spears and cut each into two or three pieces.

2. Cook the pasta according to the packet instructions, adding the asparagus pieces for the last 2 minutes. Drain the pasta and asparagus, tip into a bowl and stir in the oil to coat.

3. Pour the stock and cream into the pan, bring just to the boil, reduce the heat and stir in the pasta, asparagus and smoked salmon. Stirring, cook until piping hot, stir in the Parmesan, season if necessary and serve immediately.

Cherries and Grapes with Coconut and Raspberry Mascarpone

A simple elegant way to serve cherries and grapes. Try this recipe with other fruits, such as plums, apricots and gooseberries.

Serves 2–4

200 g/7 oz/1½ cups cherries
250 g/9 oz mascarpone cheese
150 ml/¼ pint/⅔ cup milk
3 tbsp desiccated coconut
Pinch of ground cinnamon
200 g/7 oz/1½ cups raspberries
5 tbsp soft light brown sugar
200 g/7 oz/1½ cups seedless black grapes

1. Stone (pit) the cherries, or leave them whole.

2. Spoon the mascarpone into a small bowl, stir in the milk and mix until smooth. Add the coconut, cinnamon and half of the raspberries. Mix with a fork to slightly crush the raspberries. Cover and chill until needed.

3. Pour 300 ml/½ pint/1¼ cups water in a pan and stir in the sugar. Heat until the sugar has dissolved then bring to the boil and cook for 8–10 minutes until the syrup has reduced by about one third.

4. Reduce the heat, put the cherries and grapes into the syrup and cook for 5 minutes. Add the remaining raspberries and remove from the heat. Leave the fruits in the syrup and serve hot or cold with the coconut mascarpone.

Gooseberry and Elderflower Frangipane Tart

*Tart gooseberries come in many varieties, yellow and red ones as well
as the usual green variety. In most parts of the UK you should find
elderflower blossoming at the same time as gooseberries are ripening.
Some years I've been disappointed to find they are out of sync, so I
then use elderberry syrup in place of the flowers. Serve with a dollop
of thick cream or pour over custard or natural yogurt.*

Serves 6

2–3 elderflower heads, or 1 tbsp elderflower syrup

300 g/10½ oz gooseberries

25 g/1 oz/2 tbsp butter

4 tbsp light muscovado sugar

2 medium eggs, beaten

1 tbsp plain (all-purpose) flour

60 g/2¼ oz/generous ½ cup ground almonds

A little milk, if needed

375 g/13 oz packet ready-rolled shortcrust pastry

1. Preheat the oven to 200°C, 400°F, Fan 185°C, Gas 6. If using the blossoms, shake the elderflower heads to remove any insects and pull the flowers from the stalks. Top and tail the gooseberries.

2. Put the butter and 2 tbsp of the sugar into a mixing bowl and mix together until light and fluffy.

3. Gradually beat the eggs into the mixture and stir in the flour, almonds and elderflowers or syrup. The mix should be quite stiff but add a little milk if needed.

4. Unroll the pastry and use to line a deep 20 cm/8 inch flan ring, trim any excess pastry.

5. Spread the filling in the flan case and arrange the gooseberries on top. Sprinkle over the remaining sugar.

6. Put into the hot oven and cook for 30–40 minutes until the pastry is golden and the gooseberries are soft.

Summer Fruits with Creamy Chocolate and Hazelnut Fondue

Fresh fruits, chocolate and cream – an irresistible winner. Serve with plenty of cocktail sticks for spearing the fruits, dunking into the chocolate mix and into your choice of topping.

Serves 4–6

A selection of fresh summer fruits, such as strawberries, raspberries, cherries, grapes, apricots, peaches, nectarines
200 g/7 oz plain chocolate
150 ml/¼ pint/⅔ cup double (heavy) cream
3 tbsp golden syrup
2 tbsp orange juice
50 g/1¾ oz toasted hazelnuts
A selection of topping, such as toasted coconut, crushed macaroons, crushed meringues, crushed chocolate flakes, coloured hundreds and thousands, crushed corn flakes

▶ Put the kettle on to boil. Prepare the fruit. Leave small berries whole. I prefer to leave cherries whole, but stone (pit) if necessary. Stone (pit) large fruits and cut into thick slices. Divide the fruit between plates leaving spaces in the middle for the bowls of fondue.

▶ Pour hot water (from the kettle) into a pan and place a bowl on top, making sure the base of the bowl doesn't touch the water. Heat the water but do not let it boil. Break the chocolate into the bowl and add the cream, golden syrup and orange juice. Heat gently, stirring occasionally, until the chocolate has melted and the mixture is smooth and glossy. Stir in the hazelnuts.

▶ Pour into warmed small individual bowls or coffee cups and serve immediately with the fruit and toppings.

Zabaglione with Meringue, Peaches and Loganberries

An Italian influence, perfumed peaches and the classic dessert of whisked eggs, sugar and Marsala wine. If there's time, assemble the fruit and meringue base an hour before serving so the flavours meld together.

Serves 4–6

4 ripe peaches
200 g/7 oz loganberries
6 tbsp sweet Marsala wine
2 meringue nests, about 60g
5 medium egg yolks
2 tbsp caster sugar

▶ Put the kettle on to boil. Cut the peaches in half, remove the stones (pits) and thinly slice the flesh . Put a quarter of the peach slices and half the loganberries in a small bowl and purée with a stick blender or finely chop, then stir in 1 tbsp of the Marsala.

▶ Roughly crush the meringues and divide between four to six glasses or dishes. Spoon the remaining fruits on top and pour over the fruit purée.

▶ Pour hot water (from the kettle) into a pan and place a bowl on top, making sure the base of the bowl doesn't touch the water. Heat the water but do not let it boil. Put the egg yolks, sugar and Marsala into the bowl and, with a hand-held mixer (or a balloon whisk, but this takes longer and needs stamina) whisk until it turns into a thick, creamy foam.

▶ Spoon over the fruit base and serve immediately.

Autumn/Fall

AT THIS mellow and fruitful time of the year, flavours become earthier, leaves become stronger, and fruit ripens into rich, dark colours and correspondingly intense flavours. More substantial dishes like Sausages, Black-Eye Beans and Apples with Sticky Molasses (page 134), Beef Daube with Green Tomatoes and Curly Kale (page 128) and Duck with Red Currants, Orange and Fennel (page 112) are starting to make a comeback.

This is the time of harvest festivals and horticultural shows. Pumpkins, marrows and squashes, beetroot (beet), onions and wild mushrooms, potatoes, leeks and celeriac – together these make thrilling colourful displays, and they are so tasty and enticing when served with pork, beef or duck. See Moroccan Beef (page 120), Stuffed Marrow with Smoked Sausage, Parsnip and Rice (page 132) and Spiced Potato and Pumpkin (page 108).

You may well find you have a glut of fruits gathered in from gardens, orchards or hedgerows. Remember you can turn any fruit you don't use for cooking or eating into jams and preserves for the winter and the following year. Recipes for such lovely fruits as plums, damsons and greengages, apples, blackberries and figs are included in this chapter.

Mushroom and Spinach Noodle Soup

Although available all year round, mushrooms seem to be synonymous with this season. Use a variety to give different flavours and textures.

Serves 4–6

140 g/5 oz mixed mushrooms, such as shiitake, chestnut, oyster
2 garlic cloves
Small piece of fresh root ginger
1 red chilli (see page 13)
2 shallots
Large handful of spinach leaves
1 carrot
½ lemon
2 chicken stock cubes
1 tbsp light soy sauce
140 g/5 oz vermicelli noodles

1. Put the kettle on to boil. Clean and trim the mushrooms and thinly slice. Crush the garlic and grate the ginger. Cut the chilli in half, remove the seeds and thinly slice. Halve the shallots and thinly slice with the spinach leaves. Cut the carrot into fine matchstick strips. Squeeze the juice from the lemon.

2. Pour 1.2 litres/2 pints/5 cups water (from the kettle) into a saucepan. Stir in all the ingredients except the spinach. Bring to the boil, reduce the heat and cook over a gentle heat for 15 minutes, stirring occasionally until the mushrooms and noodles are tender.

3. Tip in the spinach and cook until it wilts.

4. Serve immediately.

Celeriac and Red Onion Soup

Celeriac is a knobbly root vegetable tasting like a cross between celery and parsley. It does discolour so prepare just before using or put in water with a little lemon juice. Serve topped with a few chopped cashew nuts and hot crusty bread.

Serves 4–6

3 red onions
2 celery sticks
½ lemon
1 celeriac, about 600 g/1 lb 5 oz
1 tbsp olive oil
25 g/1 oz/2 tbsp butter
1.2 litres/2 pints/5 cups vegetable or chicken stock
1 star anise
150ml/¼ pint/²/₃ cup single (light) cream
Freshly milled salt and white pepper

▶ Finely slice the onions and chop the celery. Squeeze the juice from the lemon. Peel the celeriac and roughly chop.

▶ Heat the oil and butter in a medium pan and cook the onions until golden. Lift them out onto a plate. Add the celery and celeriac to the pan and cook gently for about 5–8 minutes until lightly browned.

▶ Add the stock, lemon juice and star anise. Bring to the boil, reduce the heat, cover and cook for 20 minutes until the celeriac is soft.

▶ Remove and discard the star anise. Whiz with a stick blender for a smooth soup or lightly crush with a potato masher.

▶ Stir in the cooked onions, reheat, add the cream and season if necessary. Serve immediately.

Sizzled Halloumi Cheese, Squash and Salsify

Salsify is a parsnip-shaped root vegetable known as the oyster plant as its flavour resembles a delicate oyster, often too subtle to notice. It's lovely in soups. You can use a parsnip as a substitute, but the flavour will be different. Halloumi is a Cypriot cheese and very useful in cooking as it holds its shape.

Serves 2

280 g/10 oz piece of squash
2 small red onions
1 root of salsify
1 tbsp lemon juice
2 red-skinned eating apples
3 tbsp shelled, unsalted peanuts
175 g/6 oz halloumi cheese
1 tbsp olive oil
1 tsp peanut oil
2 tbsp clear honey
2 tsp vegetable bouillon powder
Bunch of flat-leaved parsley
Freshly milled salt and black pepper

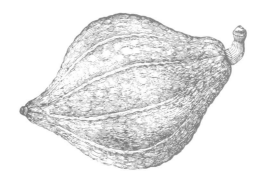

1 ▶ Peel the squash, scoop out the seeds and cut into large bite-size pieces. Halve the onions and cut into very thin slices. Peel the salsify, cut into slices and put into a bowl of water with the lemon juice. Quarter and core the apples and cut each wedge in half. Lightly crush the peanuts to break and cut the halloumi into strips.

2 ▶ Heat the olive oil in a wide shallow non-stick pan and fry the onion and squash until softened, but not browned. Stir in the peanut oil and honey and add the drained salsify, apples and halloumi. Stirring, cook for 5–6 minutes until golden and softened.

3 ▶ Mix in the bouillon powder and 4 tbsp water, the peanuts and parsley. Increase the heat and cook, stirring for 3–4 minutes until the vegetables are tender. Season if necessary and serve immediately.

Stuffed Mushroom on Pastry Tartlets with Bacon

Squares of puff pastry act as saucers for the large flat cap mushrooms with their savoury filling. Serve with a mixed leaf salad.

Serves 2

4 large flat-cap mushrooms

1 small red onion

4 streaky (fatty) bacon rashers (strips)

70 g/2½ oz cooked white rice

2 tsp freshly chopped parsley

3 tbsp grated Parmesan or mature Cheddar cheese

2 tbsp fruit chutney

375 g/13 oz packet ready-rolled puff pastry

2 tbsp olive oil

4 pitted black olives

1. Preheat the oven to 200°C, 400°F, Fan 185°C, Gas 6. Wipe the mushrooms with damp kitchen paper. Remove and finely chop the stalks, leaving the caps whole. Finely chop the onion. Cut off any bacon rind and cut the rashers (strips) into narrow strips.

2. Tip the rice into a small bowl and stir in the mushroom stalks, onion, parsley, cheese and chutney.

3. Unroll the pastry onto a lightly floured surface. Using the mushrooms as a guide, cut out four discs of pastry slightly larger. Lift the pastry discs onto a baking sheet (wrap the excess pastry, chill and use in another recipe).

4. Brush both sides of the mushrooms with a little oil and put one stalk-side uppermost on each pastry disc.

5. Spoon the rice filling into the mushroom caps, scatter over the bacon pieces and put an olive in the centre of each. Put into the hot oven and cook for about 30–40 minutes until the pastry is cooked through and the bacon crisp.

Mushroom Stroganoff

For a change, use cooked beans (flageolet or borlotti) in
place of the mushrooms. Serve as an accompaniment to
grilled (broiled) steaks or as a filling for pancakes.

Serves 4

1 onion

300 g/10½ oz mixed mushrooms, such as button, shiitake,
  chestnut, oyster

2 handfuls of celery leaves

25 g/1 oz/2 tbsp butter

1 tbsp olive oil

150 ml/¼ pint/⅔ cup vegetable stock

2 tbsp lemon juice

Pinch of saffron threads

1 tsp cornflour (cornstarch)

2 tbsp dry white wine, optional

150 ml/¼ pint/⅔ cup double (heavy) cream

2 tbsp grated Parmesan cheese

Freshly milled salt and black pepper

1. Finely chop the onion. Trim and wipe the mushrooms with damp kitchen paper. Leave any small mushrooms whole and tear larger ones into pieces. Roughly cut or tear the celery leaves.

2. Heat the butter and oil in a saucepan and cook the onion until softened but not browned. Tip in the mushrooms and cook for a few minutes until golden.

3. Pour the stock into the pan and stir in the celery leaves, lemon juice and saffron threads. Bring just to the boil and cook for 3–4 minutes until the mushrooms are cooked.

4. Blend the cornflour (cornstarch) to a paste with the wine, if using, or water, and stir into the pan. Bring to the boil and cook for 1–2 minutes.

5. Add the cream, and Parmesan, stirring once or twice until mixed. Heat through for 2–3 minutes until piping hot, season if necessary and serve immediately.

Spiced Potato and Pumpkin

An array of spices livens up any dish. Keep a good selection in your store cupboard. Serve with yogurt flavoured with a little grated onion, cucumber and seasoning.

Serves 4–6

2 large potatoes

2 sweet potatoes

300 g/10½ oz piece of pumpkin or squash

2 carrots

1 small onion

1 garlic clove

3 green cardamom pods

3 tbsp olive oil

1 tbsp mustard seeds

1 tbsp cumin seeds

½ tbsp fennel seeds

1 tsp garam masala

2 tbsp lemon juice

1 small handful of sultanas

Freshly milled salt and black pepper

1. Put the kettle on to boil. Peel and roughly chop the potatoes, sweet potatoes, pumpkin or squash and carrots. Halve the onion and cut into thin slices. Crush the garlic. Slit open and remove the seeds from the cardamom pods, discarding the husks.

2. Tip the potatoes, sweet potatoes, pumpkin or squash, and carrots into a wide shallow pan, preferably non-stick, and pour over water (from the kettle) to cover. Bring to the boil and cook for 8–10 minutes until cooked but not collapsed. Drain and wipe out the pan with kitchen paper.

3. Put the oil and onion into the pan and cook until softened. Stir in the cardamom, mustard, cumin, and fennel seeds and cook for a few seconds until they begin to 'pop'.

4. Stir the garam masala, garlic, lemon juice, sultanas and vegetables into the seeds. Stir, being careful not to let the mixture stick, until the vegetables are piping hot. Season if necessary and serve immediately.

Egg Fried Rice with Prawns (Shrimps) and Chicken

A great way of using cooked left-overs.
Serve with lemon wedges.

Serves 2–4

1 red onion
1 celery stick
Small piece of cabbage
200 g/7 oz cooked, shelled prawns (shrimps)
200 g/7 oz cooked smoked chicken
2 tbsp olive oil
25 g/1 oz/2 tbsp butter
250 g/9 oz long grain rice
2 tsp vegetable bouillon powder
2 tbsp freshly chopped parsley
Freshly milled salt and black pepper
2 medium eggs

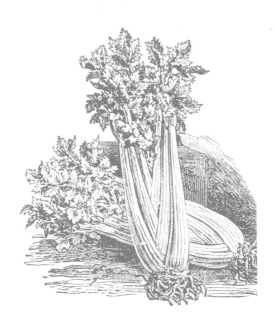

1. Put the kettle on to boil. Finely chop the onion and celery. Thinly shred the cabbage. Cut the prawns (shrimps) and chicken into small pieces.

2. Heat the oil and butter in a large pan and cook the cabbage over a high heat for 1–2 minutes until cooked and crisp. Lift out of pan with a slotted spoon and drain on kitchen paper.

3. Reduce the heat and cook the onion and celery until softened. Add the rice and cook, stirring for 2 minutes.

4. Pour 300 ml/½ pint/1¼ cups boiling water (from the kettle) into the pan and stir in the bouillon powder. Bring to the boil and cook for 12–15 minutes or until the rice is almost tender and the liquid has been absorbed. Stir in the prawns (shrimps), chicken and parsley and season if necessary. Cook until piping hot. Beat the eggs in a small bowl and quickly stir through the rice mixture – it will cook and set almost straight away. Serve topped with the crispy cabbage.

Duck with Red Currants, Orange and Fennel

*Just a few ingredients with fabulous flavour –
aniseed from the fennel, and a few redcurrants adding
tartness to give a dish that can't fail to impress.*

Serves 4

8 shallots
2 fennel bulbs
4 boneless duck breasts
300 ml/½ pint/1¼ cups chicken stock
150 ml/¼ pint/⅔ cup red wine, optional
3 tbsp orange juice
2 tsp cornflour (cornstarch)
Freshly milled salt and black pepper
4–8 strings of red currants

1. ▶ Halve the shallots, if they are large. Cut the fennel into wedges.

2. ▶ Heat a wide shallow pan and put the duck breasts skin side down then cook until browned and the fat has started to run out. Turn them over to seal the other side and remove from the pan to a plate.

3. ▶ Add the shallots and fennel to the pan, and cook until softened and lightly browned. Stir in the stock and wine, if using, (or more stock) and orange juice. Bring to the boil, reduce the heat and return the duck to the pan. Cover, and cook over a moderate heat for 20–25 minutes or until the duck is tender.

4. ▶ Remove the duck breasts, cover and keep warm. Blend the cornflour (cornstarch) to a smooth paste with a little water and stir into the pan. Bring to the boil and season to taste. Stir in the red currants and cook for a minute. Put the vegetables and sauce onto hot plates, slice each duck breast and arrange on top.

Monkfish with a Hot and Sour Sauce

One of my favourite microwave recipes, tamarind gives the sour-sweet flavour to the sauce. Use any firm-fleshed fish.

Serves 2

1 tsp tamarind paste
2 tsp light soy sauce
1 tsp chicken bouillon powder
2 tsp olive oil
Freshly milled black pepper
Two 175 g/6 oz pieces of boneless monkfish
140 g/5 oz vermicelli noodles

1. Put the kettle on to boil. In a medium microwave-proof casserole mix together the tamarind, soy sauce, bouillon powder, 4 tbsp hot water (from the kettle), oil and a little black pepper. Put the pieces of fish into the dish and turn once or twice to coat in the spicy liquid.

2. Cover and cook on High for 2–3 minutes or until the monkfish is almost cooked through. Leave to stand, covered, for 2 minutes to allow the monkfish to finish cooking.

3. Meanwhile, put the noodles into a large bowl and cover with boiling water. Leave for 2 minutes. Drain, pile into wide shallow bowls, top with the fish and spoon over the broth.

Chicken Breasts Stuffed with Prosciutto and Blue Cheese

A simple and attractive dish. Cutting through the chicken reveals the layers of filling – pak choi, prosciutto and cheese. Serve with salad leaves and chopped herbs tossed in a little nut oil and cider vinegar.

Serves 4

4 boneless chicken breasts
4 pak choi leaves
4 slices prosciutto or smoked ham
100 g/3½ oz Stilton cheese
1 tbsp sunflower oil

1. Put each chicken breast between two sheets of parchment paper, or into a freezer (food) bag, and gently press with a rolling pin to flatten them slightly. Cut a slit along the side to make a pocket or opening, but without cutting all the way through.

2. Open out the chicken and layer the pak choi leaves (folded to fit) and prosciutto or ham. Crumble a little Stilton on top and fold the chicken over the filling. Secure with wooden skewers or a piece of string.

3. Heat the oil in a wide shallow pan and cook the chicken for 10 minutes until browned on both sides, turning once.

Fragrant Chicken with Noodles, Lemon Grass and Coriander

Lemon grass looks rather like a pale spring onion (scallion) – lightly crushing with the back of a knife helps to release the sour-lemon flavour. Drop into the cooking pot and remove before serving.

Serves 4

1 leek

200 g/7 oz button mushrooms

Small bunch of coriander

1 stalk of lemon grass

1 lime

500 g/1 lb 2 oz skinless, boneless chicken fillets

350 g/12 oz flat noodles

1 tbsp sunflower oil

2 tsp sesame seed oil

1 tbsp tamarind paste

300 ml/½ pint/1¼ cups chicken stock

1 tsp paprika pepper

1. ▶ Put the kettle on to boil. Thinly slice the leek and mushrooms. Finely chop the coriander. Crush the lemon grass. Grate the rind from the lime, cut in half and squeeze the juice. Halve the chicken fillets to give 12 pieces. Put the noodles in a bowl and pour over boiling water (from the kettle) to cover.

2. ▶ Heat the sunflower oil in a heavy-based pan and fry the chicken until golden brown. Lift from the pan. Put the mushrooms and leek in the pan and cook for 2–3 minutes.

3. ▶ Return the chicken to the pan and stir in the sesame seed oil, lime rind and juice, lemon grass, tamarind paste and stock and paprika pepper. Bring just to the boil, reduce the heat and cook for about 15 minutes until the chicken is cooked through. Drain the noodles and add to the pan with the coriander. Stir to mix and serve piping hot.

Pork Goulash

*My One-Pot version of this Hungarian stew. Paprika
pepper gives the hallmark flavour to this dish. The
flavours improve if made the day before.*

Serves 4

2 onions
450 g/1 lb tomatoes or one 400 g/14 oz can of tomatoes
500 g/1 lb 2 oz boneless lean pork
1 tbsp flour
2 tsp paprika pepper
2 tbsp olive oil
300 ml/½ pint/1¼ cups vegetable stock
150 ml/¼ pint/⅔ cup red wine
1 bay leaf
2 sprigs of parsley
2 potatoes
¼ of a cauliflower
150 ml/¼ pint/⅔ cup soured cream
Freshly milled salt and black pepper

1. ▶ Thinly slice the onions. Roughly chop the tomatoes if whole. Trim the pork and cut into large bite-size pieces. Put the flour into a freezer (food) bag, add the paprika pepper and the pieces of pork and shake until the meat is coated.

2. ▶ Heat the oil in a large heavy-based pan, add the pork in small batches and cook until browned on all sides. Lift out with a slotted spoon.

3. ▶ Add the onions to the pan and cook for about 5 minutes until lightly browned, stirring occasionally.

4. ▶ Return the pork to the pan and stir in the tomatoes, stock, wine, bay leaf and parsley sprigs. Bring just to the boil, reduce the heat, cover and cook on a low heat for 1½–2 hours until the meat is very tender and cooked through.

5. ▶ Cut the potatoes into small cubes and break the cauliflower into small florets. Fifteen minutes before the end of the cooking time stir the potatoes and cauliflower into the pan. When the meat and vegetables are cooked stir in the soured cream and season if necessary.

Moroccan Beef

Ras-el-hanout is a complex Moroccan blend of herbs and spices including allspice, rosebuds and mace. This dish can be cooked on the hob as well as in the oven.

Serves 4–6

900 g/2 lb stewing beef

2 onions

2 garlic cloves

1 small turnip, about 250 g/9 oz

2 carrots

1 preserved lemon, or 1 fresh lemon

4 ready-to-eat prunes

4 ready-to-eat apricots

Large bunch of fresh coriander

2 tbsp olive oil

600 ml/1 pint/2½ cups beef stock

4–5 tsp ras-el-hanout spice blend

Freshly milled salt and black pepper

1. ▶ Preheat the oven to 160°C, 325°F, Fan 145°C, Gas 3. Trim any excess fat from the beef and cut into large, bite-size chunks. Thinly slice the onions and crush the garlic. Peel and roughly chop the turnip and slice the carrots. Cut the preserved lemon, if using, into thin strips, or, grate the rind from the lemon, cut in half and squeeze the juice. Quarter each prune and apricot. Coarsely chop the coriander.

2. ▶ Heat the oil in a large flameproof casserole, add the beef in small batches and cook for about 5 minutes, browning quickly on all sides. Lift out with a slotted spoon.

3. ▶ Add the onions to the casserole and cook for about 5 minutes until lightly browned, stirring occasionally.

4. ▶ Return the beef to the casserole and stir in the garlic, turnip, carrots, half of the coriander, the preserved lemon, or the lemon rind and juice, stock and ras-al-hanout spice blend. Heat until very hot, but not boiling. Remove from the heat.

5. ▶ Cover, put in the hot oven and cook for 1 hour. Stir in the prunes and apricots and cook for a further 30 minutes or until the meat is very tender. Stir in the remaining coriander and season if necessary.

Minced Beef with Grated Celeriac, Parsnip and Potato Topping

This dish is equally good made with lamb, chicken or pork mince in place of the beef.

Serves 6

2 large onions
2 garlic cloves
3–4 thyme sprigs
2 sweet potatoes
2 parsnips
1 small celeriac
2 tbsp olive oil
Freshly milled salt and black pepper
500 g/1 lb 2 oz lean minced (ground) beef
300 ml/½ pint/1¼ cups beef stock
400 g/14 oz can chopped tomatoes
2 tsp horseradish sauce

1. Preheat the oven to 190°C, 375°F, Fan 175°C, Gas 5. Finely chop the onions and crush the garlic. Pull the leaves from the thyme stalks.

2. Peel and coarsely grate the sweet potatoes, parsnips and celeriac. Mix in a large bowl and stir in the oil and a little seasoning.

3. Heat a flameproof shallow casserole and dry-fry the beef until browned. Lift out of the pan and drain off excess oil. Put the onion into the hot pan, and cook until softened. Return the beef to the pan and stir in the garlic, stock, tomatoes, horseradish sauce, thyme leaves and a little pepper. Bring to the boil and remove from the heat.

4. Put the vegetable mix on top of the beef – don't press it down too much. Put into the hot oven and cook for 35–40 minutes until the topping is golden and cooked through.

Mutton Shanks and Flageolet Bean Crush

Something of a classic in restaurants and bistros, here I've use flageolet beans rather than haricot beans. The beans absorb the flavours of the dish and the meat becomes very tender and falls off the bone.

Serves 4

250 g/9 oz celeriac

2 carrots

1 large onion

2 garlic cloves

3 sprigs of thyme

Two 400g/14 oz cans flageolet beans

4 mutton or lamb shanks

1 tbsp oil

450 ml/¾ pint/about 2 cups lamb or chicken stock

1 bay leaf

2 cloves

Freshly milled salt and black pepper

150 ml/¼ pint/²/₃cup low fat crème fraîche

3 tbsp freshly chopped parsley

▶ Preheat the oven to 160°C, 325°F, Fan 145°C, Gas 3. Peel and chop the celeriac, carrots and onion, and crush the garlic. Pull the thyme leaves from the stalks. Drain the cans of beans. Trim excess fat from the mutton or lamb.

▶ Heat the oil in a large flameproof casserole. Add the shanks, two at a time. Cook quickly, turning with tongs, until golden brown all over. With a slotted spoon, transfer to a plate. Repeat with the remaining two shanks.

▶ Put the celeriac, carrots, onion and garlic into the pan and cook until starting to brown. Stir in the stock, thyme, bay leaf, cloves and a little seasoning. Bring just to the boil and put the browned shanks back into the casserole.

▶ Cover, put into the hot oven and cook for 45 minutes. Stir the beans, crème fraîche and parsley into the liquid around the shanks. Cover and cook for a further 30–45 minutes until the lamb is cooked through and almost falling off the bone.

▶ To finish – put the lamb shanks onto hot plates, quickly crush the bean mixture with a potato masher or fork and spoon around the meat. Serve immediately.

Curried Puy Lentils with Beetroots (Beets) and Paneer Cheese

Puy lentils are a dark blue-green colour and are considered to have the best flavour and texture in comparison to other varieties.

Serves 4

4 ready-to-eat apricots

2 small onions

1 garlic clove

1 leek

4 small cooked beetroots (beets)

100 g/3½ oz paneer cheese

250 g/9 oz puy lentils

2 tbsp olive oil

1 tbsp korma curry powder

300 ml/½ pint/1¼ cups vegetable stock

2 tbsp pine nuts

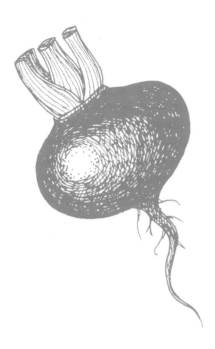

1. Thinly slice the apricots. Slice one onion and separate into rings. Finely chop the second onion and slice the garlic. Thinly slice the leek and cube the beetroots (beets). Cut the paneer cheese into small cubes or thin slices. Rinse the lentils under running cold water and drain.

2. Heat the oil in a saucepan, add the onion rings, cook until golden and with a slotted spoon lift from the pan. Put the chopped onion into the pan, add the garlic and leek and cook until starting to brown. Stir in the curry powder, drained puy lentils and pour over the stock.

3. Bring to the boil, reduce the heat and simmer for 15 minutes and stir in the apricots, beetroot (beet), pine nuts and onion rings. Cook for 10–15 minutes until the lentils are cooked but still have a 'bite'. Stir in the cheese and cook for 2–3 minutes until beginning to melt. Serve immediately.

Beef Daube with Green Tomatoes and Curly Kale

Daubes take their name from the earthenware pot they were originally cooked in, a daubière. This French dish of meat, wine, vegetables and seasonings is slowly cooked, so you can put it in the oven and forget it. You can find green tomatoes at the end of the growing season and they usually go into chutneys, but they are very tasty if fried or used in sauces.

Serves 4–6

8 green or red tomatoes

2 green chillies (see page 13)

6 curly kale leaves

500 g/1 lb 2 oz braising steak

2 tbsp olive oil

12 small onions – pickled onion size

250 g/9 oz green lentils

½ tsp turmeric powder

3 tbsp wholegrain mustard

600 ml/1 pint/2½ cups beef stock

150 ml/¼ pint/⅔ cup red wine

Small piece of cinnamon stick

Freshly milled salt and black pepper

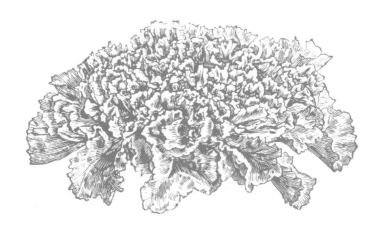

1 Preheat the oven to 180°C, 350°F, Fan 165°C, Gas 4. Quarter the tomatoes, halve the chillies, remove the seeds and thinly slice. Thinly slice the curly kale leaves. Trim the steak and cut into large bite-sized pieces.

2 Heat the oil in a large flameproof casserole and cook the steak (in batches if necessary) until browned all over. Lift out with a slotted spoon. Tip in the onions and cook until golden brown. Return the meat to the casserole and stir in the tomatoes, chillies, lentils, turmeric, mustard, stock and wine, plus the cinnamon stick. Bring just to the boil, cover and put into the hot oven. Cook for 2–2¼ hours, stirring in the curly kale after 1¾ hours, until the steak is tender. Season if necessary.

Three Cheese Cannelloni

Fresh lasagne sheets spread with a filling and rolled are the easy way to make cannelloni. I find it exasperating trying to stuff a filling into pasta tubes.

Serves 4

Oil or butter, for brushing

1 lemon

2 bunches of watercress

Handful of spinach leaves

200 g/7 oz mushrooms

3 tbsp Parmesan cheese

250 g/9 oz/1 generous cup ricotta cheese

Pinch of grated nutmeg

60 g/2¼ oz chopped walnuts

Freshly milled salt and pepper

12 fresh lasagne sheets

140 g/5 oz low-fat cream cheese

150 ml/¼ pint/⅔ cup vegetable stock

1 ► Preheat the oven to 190°C, 375°F, Fan 175°C, Gas 5. Oil or butter a shallow ovenproof dish.

2 ► Finely grate the rind from the lemon, cut in half and squeeze the juice. Pull the watercress leaves from the stalks and finely shred along with the spinach leaves. Finely chop the mushrooms and grate the Parmesan cheese.

3 ► Put the ricotta cheese into a bowl and stir in two-thirds of the grated Parmesan, the lemon rind and juice, nutmeg, watercress, spinach, mushrooms, walnuts and a little seasoning.

4 ► Place a spoonful of the mixture onto a lasagne sheet and roll up. Repeat with the remaining pasta and filling. Arrange the rolls, side by side, in the prepared dish.

5 ► Spoon the cream cheese into a bowl, stir in the stock and mix until smooth. Pour over the pasta, making sure the surface is completely covered. Sprinkle the remaining Parmesan cheese over.

6 ► Put into the hot oven and cook for about 35–45 minutes until piping hot and golden brown.

Stuffed Marrow with Smoked Sausage, Parsnip and Rice

The beauty of marrows is they come in a range of different shapes and sizes, so spread the filling thin or pile it high. You can also use this tasty filling with winter squash.

Serves 4–6

1 marrow, about 600 g/1 lb 5 oz
1 small onion
1 small parsnip
3 sprigs of celery leaves
4 parsley sprigs
200 g/7 oz cooked smoked sausage, such as breakfast sausage
60 g/2¼ oz mature hard cheese, such as Red Leicester,
  Cheddar and Double Gloucester
200 g/7 oz precooked rice
3 tbsp lemon juice
2 tsp olive oil
½ tsp ground allspice
Freshly milled salt and black pepper

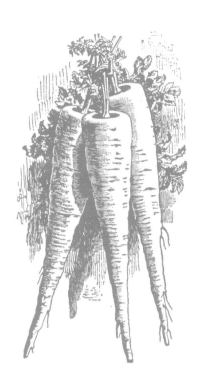

1. Preheat the oven to 190°C, 375°F, Fan 175°C, Gas 5. Cut the marrow in half lengthways and scoop out the seeds and fibre. Finely chop the onion, parsnip, celery leaves and parsley. Cut the sausage into small cubes. Coarsely grate the cheese.

2. Put the chopped vegetables and herbs into a bowl and stir in the rice, sausage, lemon juice, oil, allspice and a little seasoning.

3. Put the marrow halves side by side in a shallow ovenproof dish. Fill with the rice mixture and scatter over the cheese.

4. Put into the hot oven and cook for 30–40 minutes until tender, removing the foil for the last 10 minutes for the top to brown.

Sausages, Black-Eye Beans and Apples with Sticky Molasses

Cooler, chilly days call for a smoky sausage dish to share with friends and family. The recipe easily doubles to serve a crowd. Serve with ketchup, onion chutney and lots of crusty bread.

Serves 4–6

2 red onions

2 leeks

10 sausages, choose a selection of your favourites

3 red eating apples

410 g/14 oz can black-eyed beans

2 tsp olive oil

300 ml/½ pint/1¼ cups vegetable stock

2 tsp red wine vinegar

3 tbsp wholegrain mustard

1 tbsp molasses or black treacle

½ tsp smoky paprika pepper

1 ▶ Halve the onions and thinly slice. Finely slice the leeks. Cut the sausages in half. Quarter the apples, remove and discard the core, and cut each quarter into two wedges. Drain and wash the beans.

2 ▶ Heat the oil in a large shallow, non-stick frying pan and cook all the sausage pieces for a few minutes until the juices begin to flow and they are lightly browned. Stir in the onion and cook until golden and the sausages almost cooked.

3 ▶ Add the stock, leeks, apples, beans, vinegar, mustard, molasses or treacle and paprika. Bring just to the boil, reduce the heat and cook for 10 minutes, stirring occasionally until cooked.

Turkey and Mushrooms with Potato Gnocchi

Gnocchi are small dumplings made from potatoes and eggs.

Serves 4

1 leek
200 g/7 oz mushrooms
350 g/12 oz skinless turkey breast meat
2 tsp sunflower oil
4 tbsp cranberries
3 sage leaves
400 ml/14 fl oz/1⅔ cups chicken stock
Freshly milled salt and black pepper
500 g/1 lb 2 oz ready-made fresh potato gnocchi
3 tbsp freshly grated pecorino cheese

1. Put the kettle on to boil. Thinly slice the leek. Trim and roughly chop the mushrooms. Cut the turkey into very thin strips.

2. Heat the oil in a large pan and cook the turkey until browned and almost cooked. Stir in the leek, mushrooms, cranberries, and the sage leaves torn into pieces. Stir in 200 ml/7 fl oz/about 1 cup of the stock and cook until the turkey is tender. Remove the mixture to a bowl.

3. Pour boiling water (from the kettle) into the pan, add a little salt, tip in the gnocchi and boil for 2 minutes. The gnocchi will rise to the surface of the pan. Then drain.

4. Heat the pan, return the turkey mixture to the pan, pour in the remaining stock, bring just to the boil and stir in the hot gnocchi. Stir and heat until the turkey and gnocchi are piping hot.

5. Stir in the cheese and season if necessary. Serve immediately.

Vegetarian Hotpot

*A useful dish for those not wanting to have meat in their diet
but still wanting the shapes and textures of meat.*

Serves 4

1 small onion
1 garlic clove
4 sprigs of thyme
100 g/3½ oz paneer cheese
1 large potato
2 large parsnips
150 ml/¼ pint/⅔ cup crème fraîche
1 tsp Madras curry paste
150 ml/¼ pint/⅔ cup vegetable stock
2 large handfuls of spinach leaves
350 g/12 oz cubes of 'meat' substitute
Freshly milled salt and black pepper
2 tsp sunflower oil

▶ Preheat the oven to 200°C, 400°F, Fan 185°C, Gas 6. Finely chop the onion and the garlic. Pull the leaves from the thyme and grate the cheese. Thinly slice the potato and parsnips.

▶ Spoon the crème fraîche into an ovenproof dish and stir in the curry paste, onion, garlic, stock and thyme leaves. Fold in the spinach leaves, 'meat' substitute and a little black pepper.

▶ Top with overlapping slices of potato and parsnip, season, brush with oil and scatter over the cheese.

▶ Put into the hot oven and cook for 35–45 minutes or until golden brown and cooked through.

Plums, Damsons and Greengages Poached in a Rosemary Syrup

Rosemary adds an unusual delicate flavour to this season's fruits.

Serves 4

300 g/10½ oz plums
200 g/7 oz greengages
200 g/7 oz damsons
2 cardamom pods
2 sprigs of mint
Small sprig of rosemary
100 g/3½ oz soft brown sugar

1. Put the kettle on to boil. Remove any stalks from the fruits. Halve the fruits and remove the stones (pits). Make a small slit in each cardamom pod.

2. Pour 150 ml/¼ pint/⅔ cup water into a wide shallow pan. Stir in the cardamom, mint, rosemary and sugar. Bring to the boil and cook for 5 minutes.

3. Reduce the heat and spoon the fruits into the hot syrup. Cook gently for 5–10 minutes, turning once, until the fruits are just soft and hold their shape.

4. Serve hot or cold.

Apple Pie with a Nutty, Lemon, Cinnamon and Cream Cheese Filling

A pastry topped pie. The lemony cream cheese filling melts to give a surprising sauce around the apples. Hazel nuts, macadamia nuts or pecans can replace the peanuts.

Serves 4–6

Butter

1 lemon

1 lime

600 g/1 lb 5 oz cooking apples, such as Bramley's

70 g/2½ oz caster sugar, plus 1 tbsp

100 g/3½ oz low-fat cream cheese

½ tsp ground cinnamon

70 g/2½ oz chopped walnuts

Milk, for brushing

375 g/13 oz packet ready-rolled shortcrust pastry

1. ▶ Preheat the oven to 200°C, 400°F, Fan 185°C, Gas 6. Lightly butter a 850 ml/1½ pint/3½ cup capacity pie dish or shallow dish.

2. ▶ Halve the lemon and squeeze the juice. Finely grate the rind from the lime, cut in half and squeeze the juice. Peel, core and thinly slice the apples. Put the apples into a bowl and stir in the lemon juice and sugar, reserving 1 tbsp.

3. ▶ Put the cream cheese into a small bowl and add the cinnamon, walnuts, lime rind and juice, mix well.

4. ▶ Tip half the fruit into the dish and, spoon over the cheese mixture and cover with the remaining fruit.

5. ▶ Brush the edges of the dish with a little milk. Unroll the pastry and place over the filling. Press and pinch the pastry around the edges of the dish and trim the excess. Make a small knife cut in the top of the pastry to allow any steam to escape. Brush with a little milk and sprinkle over the reserved sugar.

6. ▶ Put into the hot oven and cook for 30–40 minutes until the pastry is golden and the fruit is tender.

Bramble and Grape Spiced Batter Pudding

Warming, comforting pudding of my childhood, after picking hedgerow berries. Serve with yogurt or single (light) cream.

Serves 4–6

300 g/10½ oz brambles or blackberries
300 g/10½ oz seedless grapes, black or green
140 g/5 oz plain (all-purpose) flour
¼ tsp ground cinnamon
¼ tsp ground mixed spice
4 medium eggs
450 ml/16 fl oz/about 2 cups skimmed milk
2 tbsp clear honey
Butter
115 g/4 oz/½ cup soft brown sugar
Icing sugar, to sift

1. Carefully remove any stalks from the brambles or blackberries and halve the grapes.

2. Sift the flour, cinnamon and mixed spice into a mixing bowl. With a coil or balloon whisk beat in the eggs, milk and honey. Mix until smooth – cover and chill until required.

3. Preheat the oven to 190°C, 375°F, Fan 175°C, Gas 5.

4. Butter a shallow ovenproof dish (large enough to hold the fruit in a single layer). Arrange the fruit in the dish and sprinkle over the sugar. Whisk the batter and pour over the fruit.

5. Put into the hot oven and cook for 30–40 minutes until cooked and golden. Sift over a little icing sugar and serve immediately.

Wine Poached Figs with Mascarpone and Meringue Cream

An elegant dessert and so easy to prepare.

Serves 2

4 fresh figs

50 g/1¾ oz butter

300 ml/½ pint/1¼ cups red wine

150 ml/¼ pint/²/₃ cup orange juice

2 tbsp clear honey

2–3 drops vanilla extract

4 tbsp mascarpone cheese

2 tbsp milk

1 meringue nest

1. Cut the figs in half from the stalk to the base.

2. Melt the butter in a small pan or frying pan and stir in the wine, orange juice, honey and vanilla extract. Bring just to the boil and cook for 5–8 minutes to concentrate the flavours.

3. With a spoon carefully put the figs into the liquid and gently cook for 15 minutes or until tender.

4. Put the mascarpone into a small bowl, stir in the milk and crumble in the meringue nest. Serve on top of the figs.

Winter

THE DEPTH of winter demands hearty fare: game of all varieties (venison, pheasant, guinea fowl and rabbit), loin of pork and whole stuffed fish, not to mention stalks, stems, roots and tubers of many kinds. Every season has an abundance of produce and winter is no exception. Just try, by way of example, Guinea Fowl with Thyme and Grapes (page 182), Venison and Juniper Cassoulet (page 176) or, Pumpkin and Sweet Potato Rösti (page 156).

It's always good to make the most of comforting winter vegetables, such as parsnips, carrots, kale, red cabbage and winter greens. And I've rung the changes on the typical ingredients of our mid-winter festivities. Brussels sprouts, turkey, cranberries, chestnuts and walnuts, pears, prunes, mandarin oranges and heavy sticky puddings can all be found here in such new guises as Turkey, Cranberries, Chestnut and Wheat (page 178), Beef and Prawn (Shrimp) Parcels with a Dipping Sauce (page 148) and Mandarin Orange, Ginger and Walnut Upside-Down Pudding (page 185).

After the bitter, icy blasts of a December or January snowstorm, what could be more welcoming?

Squash, Chestnut and Pancetta Soup

A warming soup enhanced with the flavour of cardamom. As well as fresh, chestnuts are available canned, frozen or vacuum-packed. To peel fresh chestnuts, make a small nick in the skins, put into a bowl of boiling water and leave for 5 minutes. Carefully remove and, when cool enough to handle, peel with a sharp knife. Serve with a swirl of thick Greek yogurt or cream and crusty rolls.

Serves 4–6

350 g/12 oz wedge of squash
1 leek
2 garlic cloves
5 pancetta slices
1 tbsp sunflower oil
¼ tsp ground cardamom
1.2 litres/2 pints/5 cups chicken or vegetable stock
250 g/9 oz shelled chestnuts
1 tbsp wholegrain mustard
2 tbsp freshly chopped parsley
Freshly milled black pepper

1. Cut the thick peel off the squash, remove any seeds and roughly chop. Thinly slice the leek and finely chop the garlic.

2. Heat a large saucepan and dry-fry the pancetta slices until cooked and crisp. Lift onto a plate.

3. Add the oil, leek, squash, garlic and cardamom to the pan, cook gently for about 5 minutes, stirring occasionally, until beginning to soften but not brown.

4. Pour the stock into the pan and stir in the chestnuts, mustard and half the parsley. Bring just to the boil, reduce the heat and cook gently for 15–20 minutes until the chestnuts are tender.

5. Using a stick blender, whiz until fairly smooth. Crumble the pancetta into the soup, stir in the remaining parsley, season if necessary, reheat and serve immediately.

Curried Parsnip and Carrot Soup

*Give this silky velvety soup more heat by using a
hotter curry paste. Serve with hot naan breads.*

Serves 4–6.

1 small onion
2 parsnips
2 carrots
1 garlic clove
Small piece of fresh ginger
1 tbsp olive oil
1.2 litres/2 pints/5 cups vegetable stock
2 tbsp mild curry paste
3 tbsp freshly chopped coriander
150 ml/¼ pint/⅔ cup coconut milk
Freshly milled salt and black pepper

1▶ Roughly chop the onion, parsnips and carrots. Crush the garlic and
grate the ginger.

2▶ Heat the oil in a large saucepan and add the onion, parsnips and
carrots, cook gently for about 5–8 minutes, stirring occasionally,
until just starting to brown.

3▶ Pour the stock into the pan, stir in the garlic, ginger, curry paste and
half the coriander. Bring just to the boil, reduce the heat and cook
gently for 15–20 minutes until the vegetables are soft.

4▶ Using a stick blender, whiz until fairly smooth. Stir in the coconut
milk and remaining coriander, season if necessary, bring back to the
boil and serve immediately.

Ham and Mustard Savoury Bread Pudding

Sandwiches in a savoury custard — simple and with numerous variations. Serve with winter salad leaves.

Serves 2–4

Butter
4 slices, lean, cooked, smoked ham
3 tomatoes
2 pickled onions
8 slices olive bread, about 250 g/9 oz
2 tbsp wholegrain mustard
8 small spinach leaves
3 large eggs
600 ml/1 pint/2½ cups milk
2 tsp liquid vegetable stock
Freshly milled black pepper

1. Lightly butter a shallow ovenproof dish. Trim any fat from the ham. Slice the tomatoes and onions.

2. Generously butter one side of the bread slices. Spread four slices with mustard and top with spinach leaves, ham, tomatoes and onions. Cover with the remaining bread, butter side down to make sandwiches. Lightly butter the top surface of the sandwiches and cut each in half.

3. Arrange the sandwiches, overlapping and at an angle, in the dish.

4. In a small bowl mix together the eggs and milk, then strain into a jug. Stir in the stock and a little black pepper and pour over the bread. Leave to stand for 30 minutes.

5. Preheat the oven to 180°C, 350°F, Fan 165°C, Gas 4.

6. Put the dish into the hot oven and bake for 45–55 minutes until cooked and golden. Serve hot.

Beef and Prawn (Shrimp) Parcels with a Dipping Sauce

Rather like spring rolls, delicious nibbles with a dipping sauce, or for a light meal serve with salad and coleslaw. Be careful using fresh horseradish, the pungent root is very strong and gives mega heat to any dip. Give a prize to anyone who realizes Brussels sprouts are in the filling, or use shredded spinach if you prefer.

Serves 4–6 as nibbles or 2 as a light meal

1 medium egg
1 shallot
6 Brussels sprouts
140 g/5 oz cooked shelled prawns (shrimps), thawed if frozen
200 g/7 oz rump or fillet beef steak
2 tbsp freshly chopped parsley
1 tsp cornflour (cornstarch)
Freshly ground black pepper
6 sheets of filo pastry, thawed if frozen
Sunflower oil, for brushing
Sesame seeds

Dipping sauce
2 tbsp tomato ketchup
150 ml/¼ pint/⅔ cup mayonnaise
Pinch of freshly grated horseradish, or 1 tsp horseradish sauce

 Preheat the oven to 190°C, 375°F, Fan 175°C, Gas 5. Break the egg in a small bowl and beat. Finely chop the shallot, trim and finely shred the Brussels sprouts. Roughly chop the prawns (shrimps). Trim any fat from the beef, finely slice and put into a mixing bowl.

 Add the prawns (shrimps), shallot, Brussels sprouts, parsley, cornflour (cornstarch) and pepper to taste and mix well.

 Unroll the filo pastry, keeping it covered with clear film (plastic wrap) until needed. Working quickly brush a pastry sheet with a little oil, cover with another sheet and brush with oil. Cut into 13 cm/5 inch squares. Put a spoonful of filling on each pastry square, brush the edges with egg, fold in the sides a little and roll the pastry over the filling. Lift onto a baking sheet. Repeat with the remaining pastry and filling. Brush the rolls with a little oil and scatter over some sesame seeds.

 Put into the hot oven and cook for 25–35 minutes until crisp and golden.

 Mix all the dip ingredients together in a small bowl and serve with the piping hot parcels.

Jamaican Jerk Chicken with Winter Salad

Good quality spice mixes are a quick way of adding flavours to meat or fish. The winter salad is a coleslaw of vegetables, fresh and dried fruits and nuts folded into thick yogurt.

Serves 4–6

450 g/1 lb skinless chicken fillets
1–2 tsp jerk seasoning
2 tsp sunflower oil

Salad
300 ml/½ pint/1¼ cups thick Greek yogurt
2 tsp lemon juice
2 tbsp toasted sesame seeds
3 heaped tbsp walnut pieces
Small handful of sultanas
1 small red onion
¼ small white cabbage, about 140 g/5 oz
¼ small red cabbage, about 140 g/5 oz
1 large carrot
2 celery stalks
1 eating apple
Freshly milled salt and black pepper

Warm wraps and rolls and tomato relish, to serve

1. ► Cut the chicken into thin slices. Put the jerk seasoning and oil into a bowl and stir in the chicken until coated. Leave to marinade for 1–2 hours, or just 15 minutes – it will make a difference to the flavour.

2. ► Prepare the salad. Spoon the yogurt into a bowl and stir in the lemon juice, sesame seeds, walnut pieces and sultanas.

3. ► Finely shred or coarsely grate the onion, red and white cabbage and carrot. Thinly slice the celery. Cut the apple in half, core and grate. Stir the vegetables and apple into the yogurt dressing. Season with salt and pepper.

4. ► Cook the chicken under a hot grill or in a hot griddle pan until browned and cooked through, turning once. Spoon the salad into hot wraps or rolls, top with the chicken and add a dollop of relish.

Hot Beef and Beans with Radicchio and Chicory Salad

A big bold salad with the slightly bitter leaves of radicchio and chicory.

Serves 2 as a main meal or 4 as a starter

2 heads of chicory

½ a radicchio

2 sirloin beef steaks

1 garlic clove

2 slices sourdough bread

1 tbsp tomato purée

Olive oil, for frying

2 tsp lemon juice

1 tbsp red wine vinegar

1 tbsp wholegrain mustard

Freshly milled black pepper

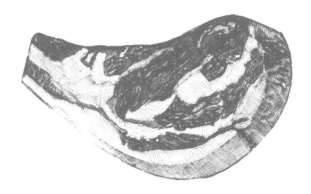

1 ▶ Divide the chicory and radicchio heads into leaves and put onto plates. Trim any excess fat from the steak. Crush the garlic.

2 ▶ Rub the slices of bread with crushed garlic, tomato purée and a little oil.

3 ▶ Heat a little oil in a wide heavy-based griddle pan and cook the steak for 2–3 minutes either side, or longer if you prefer them cooked through. At the same time cook the bread slices until crisp and browned on both sides. Lift from the pan and cut the steaks into slices and roughly cube the bread and scatter over the leaves.

4 ▶ Pour the lemon juice and wine vinegar and spoon the mustard into the hot pan juices and quickly bring to the boil, scraping up any sediment, and drizzle over the salads. Serve immediately.

Lasagne with Mushrooms, Squash and Chard

Not a traditional lasagne, rather a simplified version. A mass of vegetables are used but put your own favourite selection together from your veg-box. Serve on its own with garlic bread and salad or add a steak or chop. Uses both the hob and the oven but worth the wait.

Serves 4–6

100 g/3½ oz mature Cheddar cheese

60 g/2¼ oz Parmesan cheese

250 g/9 oz/1 generous cup ricotta cheese

150 ml/¼ pint/⅔ cup milk

Freshly milled salt and black pepper

1 lemon

1 small onion

2 garlic cloves

500 g/1 lb 2 oz mixed vegetables: mushrooms, pumpkin or winter squash, cauliflower, radicchio, spinach and chard

2 tbsp olive oil

300 ml/½ pint/1¼ cups vegetable stock

150 ml/¼ pint/⅔ cup passata (sieved tomatoes)

1 tsp harissa sauce

12 fresh lasagne sheets

1. Preheat the oven to 190°C, 375°F, Fan 175°C, Gas 5. Grate the Cheddar and Parmesan cheeses, keep them separate. Spoon the ricotta cheese into a bowl, mix in the milk and seasoning until smooth and stir in half the grated Cheddar cheese. Grate the lemon, cut in half and squeeze the juice. Finely chop the onion, crush the garlic and slice the mushrooms. Peel the pumpkin or squash and roughly dice. Break the cauliflower into small florets and shred the radicchio, spinach and chard.

2. Heat the oil in a wide flameproof casserole and cook the onion and garlic until softened. Tip in the mushrooms and the rest of the vegetables and stir in the hot oil until softened. Stir in the stock, lemon rind and juice, passata, harissa and seasoning. Bring to the boil and cook for 10 minutes. Remove from the heat.

3. Spoon half of the mixture into a bowl. Pour about one-third of the cheese mixture over the vegetables in the casserole, then cover with half of the lasagne sheets. Spoon the reserved vegetable mixture over, add a third of the cheese mixture, then cover with half of the lasagne sheets. Cover with the cheese mixture and scatter over the remaining grated Cheddar cheese and the Parmesan cheese.

4. Put into the hot oven and cook for about 35–45 minutes until golden brown and cooked through.

Pumpkin and Sweet Potato Rösti

A Swiss potato 'cake'. Could be made with potato and parsnip. Winter squash and pumpkins have tough thick skins so they can be stored throughout the winter. It can be cooked in a hot oven. Serve with roasts, or make into individual cakes and top with a poached egg. This is a lovely accompaniment to goose.

Serves 4

700 g/1 lb 9 oz piece of pumpkin
2 large carrots
1 sweet potato
½ tsp ground allspice
½ tsp ground ginger
Freshly milled black pepper
3 tbsp butter
2 tbsp olive oil

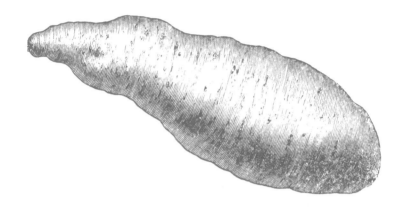

1. Peel the skin from the pumpkin and with a spoon scrape out and discard the seeds.

2. Coarsely grate the pumpkin, carrots and sweet potato and put into a large bowl.

3. Stir in the ground allspice and ginger and a little black pepper.

4. Heat half of the butter and oil in a large non-stick frying pan. Tip the vegetables into the hot pan, spread into a single layer and press firmly.

5. Cover and cook over a medium heat for 15–20 minutes until the bottom is golden and the vegetables cooked. Slide out onto a flat plate. Heat the remaining butter and oil and slide the vegetable 'cake' back into the pan. Cook for a further 10–15 minutes until the base is golden and the vegetables are cooked. Cut into wedges and serve piping hot.

Vegetable Risotto

*Quick risotto, there's usually a separate pan of stock
bubbling away but here all the flavours are in the pan
and I've used boiling water from the kettle to simplify
the process. Serve with extra Parmesan. Cooked shellfish,
or different types of meat, or mushrooms can be added.*

Serves 4

1 large onion
1 garlic clove
2 parsnips
Small wedge of cabbage
4 sage leaves
2 tbsp olive oil
25 g/1 oz/2 tbsp butter
250 g/9 oz risotto rice, such as arborio, baldo or carnaroli
150 ml/¼ pint/⅔ cup dry white wine or dry vermouth
2 tsp vegetable or chicken bouillon powder, or use stock cubes
Pinch of saffron threads, optional
3 tbsp Parmesan cheese
2 tbsp chopped fresh parsley
Freshly milled salt and black pepper

1 Put the kettle on to boil. Finely chop the onion and crush the garlic. Coarsely grate the parsnips and finely shred the cabbage. Tear the sage leaves in half.

2 Put the oil, butter and onion into a large pan and cook over a medium heat until softened but not browned.

3 Add the garlic and rice and, stirring, cook for about 2 minutes. Add the wine or vermouth and cook until absorbed. Stir in the parsnips, cabbage and sage leaves.

4 Pour 300 ml/½ pint/1¼ cups hot water (from the kettle) into the pan and stir in the bouillon powder or stock cubes and saffron, if using. Stir occasionally to prevent sticking until the liquid has been absorbed. Repeat this process once more until you have added about 600 ml/1 pint/2½ cups water in total. The rice should be cooked and creamy, but still retain a slight bite. Expect this to take about 20 minutes.

5 Stir in the Parmesan cheese and parsley, season lightly and serve piping hot.

Ginger and Lemon Fish

Choose a sustainable fish. Ask your fishmonger to clean it and remove the head if you prefer, and make sure it will fit your tin.

Serves 4

2 large handfuls of spinach leaves
½ lemon
2 cm/¾ inch piece of fresh ginger
55 g/2 oz/¼ cup butter
½ tsp ground lemon myrtle
Freshly milled black pepper
1.5 kg/3 lb 5 oz whole fish, such as sea bass or salmon (see note above)
3 tbsp dry white wine
150 ml/¼ pint/⅔ cup fish or vegetable stock

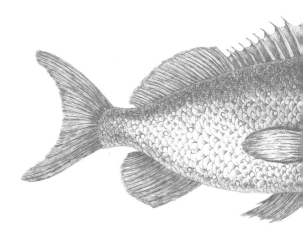

1. Put the kettle on to boil. Preheat the oven to 190°C, 375°F, Fan 175°C, Gas 5. Put the spinach leaves into a large bowl and pour over boiling water (from the kettle) to cover. Leave for 5–7 minutes for the leaves to wilt, then drain in a sieve and press or squeeze out as much water as possible.

2. Finely grate the rind from the lemon and squeeze the juice. Cut the ginger into fine shreds.

3. Put the butter into a small bowl and mix in the lemon rind and juice, lemon myrtle, ginger and black pepper.

4. Wash and dry the fish with kitchen paper. Make 4–5 diagonal cuts on one side of the fish.

5. Push the spinach into the cavity of the fish and put blobs of the butter mix on top of the spinach – use half. Spread the remaining butter mix into the cuts on the top of the fish.

6. Lift the fish onto a shallow roasting tin and pour the wine and stock over the top. Cover and put into the hot oven and cook for 20 minutes. Remove the cover and cook for a further 5–10 minutes until the fish is cooked through – this depends on the thickness of the fish.

7. Serve the fish with any liquid spooned over.

Pheasant with Spiced Red Cabbage

Game and spicy vegetables make a warming winter casserole.

Serves 4

2 oven-ready pheasants
4 smoked bacon rashers (strips)
8 shallots
3 carrots
250 g/9 oz red cabbage
1 eating apple
1 tbsp sunflower oil
4 sprigs of thyme
600 ml/1 pint/2½ cups game or chicken stock
150 ml/¼ pint/⅔ cup sweet cider
2 tsp red wine vinegar
2 tsp cornflour (cornstarch)
Freshly milled salt and black pepper

1. ▶ Preheat the oven to 190°C, 375°F, Fan 175°C, Gas 5.

2. ▶ Cut each pheasant into four pieces. Remove the bacon rinds (strips) and chop the rashers.

3. ▶ Cut the shallots in half. Slice the carrots and red cabbage. Quarter, core and chop the apple.

4. ▶ Heat the oil in a flameproof casserole, and brown the pheasant portions all over – it may be easier to cook them in two batches. Lift out with tongs onto a plate. Add the bacon, shallots and carrots and cook for 5 minutes until beginning to brown.

5. ▶ Remove from the heat. Stir in the cabbage and apple, arrange the pheasant portions on top of the vegetables, add the thyme sprigs and pour over the stock, cider and red wine vinegar.

6. ▶ Cover, put into the hot oven and cook for 50 minutes. In a small bowl mix the cornflour (cornstarch) to a paste with a little water. Remove the casserole from the oven and stir in the paste. Cover and return to the oven for 15 minutes or until the pheasant is tender and the juices have thickened, season if necessary.

Rabbit Portions and Vegetables with Wholegrain Mustard Sauce

Rustic wintry dish, a meal in itself, just needs crunchy bread to mop up the juices. Serve the rabbit joints on the vegetables with the mustardy juices spooned over.

Serves 4

- 4 rashers (strips) smoked streaky (fatty) bacon
- 1 large onion
- 3 carrots
- Small piece of turnip, about 200 g/7 oz
- 6 kale leaves
- 1 tbsp plain (all-purpose) flour
- ½ tsp ground mace
- Freshly milled salt and black pepper
- 4 rabbit joints
- 2 tbsp sunflower oil
- 300 ml/½ pint/1¼ cups chicken or vegetable stock
- 4 tbsp wholegrain mustard

1▶ Remove the bacon rinds and slice. Finely chop the onion and slice the carrots. Peel the turnip and cut into small cubes. Thinly slice the kale leaves.

2▶ Mix the flour, mace and seasoning in a food (freezer) bag. Add the rabbit joints and shake until thoroughly coated.

3▶ Heat the oil in a flameproof pan and put the rabbit in a single layer, and cook until browned each side. Lift out onto a plate.

4▶ Add the onion and bacon to the pan and cook until lightly browned. Return the rabbit to the pan, pour over the stock and stir in mustard. Cover and cook for 20 minutes, stirring occasionally.

5▶ Stir in the carrots, turnip and kale, then cook for 15 minutes or until the rabbit is cooked through and the vegetables are tender.

Slow-Cooked Pork in Milk

An unusual method of cooking pork, but traditional
in parts of Italy. Long slow cooking of pork
submerged in milk results in tender flavoursome meat
and lots of brown curds from the milk.

Serves 6–8

1 small onion

2 carrots

2 garlic cloves

½ lemon

1 tbsp oil

55 g/2 oz/¼ cup butter

1.3 kg/3 lb boned, rolled pork loin, skin and fat removed

2 sage leaves

1 small cinnamon stick

Freshly milled salt and black pepper

1.2 litres/2 pints/5 cups full-fat milk

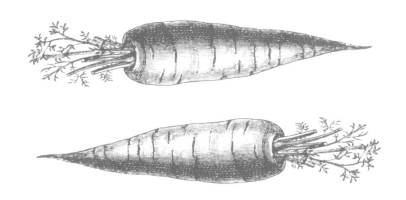

1. Finely chop the onion and carrots and crush the garlic. Peel the rind from the lemon in large pieces and squeeze the juice.

2. Heat the oil and butter in a large heavy-based pan and brown the meat all over. Remove and cook the onion and carrots until just beginning to brown. Return the pork to the pan and add the garlic, lemon peel and juice, sage, cinnamon and seasoning. Pour the milk over the meat to cover. Half cover with the lid and cook over a gentle heat for 2½–3 hours until the meat is almost falling apart and the milk has reduced to brown curds – add more milk if it becomes too dry.

3. Lift the meat onto a plate and slice or tear into large pieces. Remove the cinnamon stick and lemon rind and with a fork or potato masher lightly crush the vegetables.

4. Spoon the crushed vegetables and curds onto plates or wide shallow bowls and put the pork on top.

Pork, Sage and Mixed Beans

Various beans can be used, such as black eyed beans, black turtle beans, butter beans, haricot beans, lima beans, pinto beans, red kidney beans, rose cocoa beans, alubia beans and mung beans. Don't season beans until the end as salt toughens them.

Serves 4–6

350 g/12 oz mixed dried beans

1 large onion

2 carrots

½ turnip

½ Savoy cabbage

Small bunch of parsley

500 g/1 lb 2 oz boneless pork

300 ml/½ pint/1¼ cups unsweetened apple juice

5 sage leaves

Freshly milled black pepper

1 vegetable stock cube

1. ▶ Put the beans into a large bowl, cover with cold water and leave to soak overnight.

2. ▶ Roughly chop the onion, carrots and turnip. Cut the cabbage into wedges and finely chop the parsley. Cut the pork into large bite-size pieces.

3. ▶ Drain the beans, put into a heavy-based saucepan, cover with cold water and boil for 35 minutes and drain.

4. ▶ Wipe out the pan with kitchen paper and fry the pork until golden. Lift out of the pan, drain off any excess fat and cook the onion until browned. Return the beans and pork to the pan. Stir in the turnip, carrots, apple juice, 300 ml/½ pint/1¼ cups water, sage leaves, half of the parsley and black pepper. Bring just to the boil, reduce the heat, cover and cook for 20 minutes. Crumble the stock cube into the pan and stir in the cabbage. Cook for a further 15–25 minutes until the beans are tender and the pork is cooked through. Stir in the remaining parsley before serving.

Turkey Saltimbocca

There's a lot of well-flavoured turkey around at this time of year. Thin turkey slices are topped with sage leaves, prosciutto and lemon slices, all secured with a cocktail stick. This Italian dish is traditionally made with veal – use English rose veal.

Serves 2

½ radicchio
2 turkey slices, about 150 g/5½ oz each
2 slices prosciutto
2 sage leaves
2 lemon slices
1 tbsp plain (all-purpose) flour
Freshly milled salt and black pepper
250 g/9 oz rice noodles
1 tbsp olive oil
25 g/1 oz/2 tbsp butter
150 ml/¼ pint/⅔ cup dry white wine
3 tbsp chicken stock

2 wooden cocktail sticks

1. ► Put the kettle on to boil. Separate the radicchio leaves, tear if large.

2. ► Put each turkey slice between two pieces of clear film (plastic wrap) and roll with a rolling pin to a thickness of about 5 mm/¼ inch.

3. ► Put a slice of prosciutto on top of each turkey slice, folding it over to fit. Put a sage leaf on top and cover with a lemon slice. Secure with a wooden cocktail stick.

4. ► Put the flour onto a plate, season and dust over the meat. Put the noodles into a large bowl and pour over boiling water, to cover.

5. ► Heat the oil and butter in a frying pan. Cook the turkey for 3–4 minutes on each side until golden brown and cooked through.

6. ► Put the radicchio into the pan, pour over the wine and chicken stock and quickly cook until the radicchio has wilted and the sauce thickened a little.

7. ► Drain the hot noodles and serve with the saltimbocca, radicchio and sauce.

Game Casserole with Root Vegetables

Packs of diced game are available from many butchers and supermarkets. The root vegetables thicken the juices. Serve in bowls with corn chips or crisps on the side.

Serves 2

350 g/12 oz boneless game, such as grouse, pheasant,
  partridge, rabbit
1 red onion
2 garlic cloves
2 carrots
2 parsnips
4 Jerusalem artichokes
2 potatoes
Bunch of parsley
1 tbsp plain (all-purpose) flour
1 tbsp olive oil
600 ml/1 pint/2½ cups game or chicken stock
4 juniper berries
1 bay leaf
1 tbsp grated orange rind
Freshly milled salt and black pepper

 Trim the game and cut into bite-sized pieces. Finely chop the onion and garlic. Slice the carrots, parsnips and artichokes. Cube the potatoes and finely chop the parsley. Put the flour in a food (freezer) bag. Add the pieces of game and shake until thoroughly coated.

 Heat the oil in a wide non-stick pan and brown the game pieces – it may be easier to cook them in two batches. Lift out with tongs onto a plate. Add the onion and garlic and cook for 3–5 minutes until beginning to soften.

 Return the game to the pan. Pour over the stock and stir in the carrots, juniper berries, bay leaf, orange rind and half the chopped parsley. Cover, and cook for 20 minutes, stirring occasionally. Stir in the parsnips, artichokes and potatoes. Cover and cook for a further 20 minutes until the game is tender and the vegetables are cooked. Season if necessary, stir in the remaining parsley and serve immediately.

Gammon Steaks with Winter Greens and Cider

Use smoked or unsmoked gammon steaks, as preferred. Cider, orange, brown sugar and Dijon mustard give a syrupy glaze to the meat.

Serves 2

1 eating apple

¼ small Savoy cabbage

Handful of Brussels sprouts

½ orange

2 gammon steaks, about 140 g/5 oz each

2 tsp olive oil

150 ml/¼ pint/⅔ cup ham or chicken stock

150 ml/¼ pint/⅔ cup dry cider, optional or extra stock

Freshly milled black pepper

½ tsp Dijon mustard

1 tbsp soft brown sugar

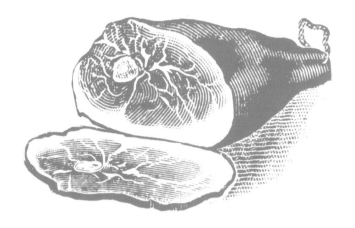

1. Halve the apple, core and cut into wedges. Thinly slice the cabbage and Brussels sprouts. Grate the rind from the orange and squeeze the juice. Snip the gammon rind at intervals.

2. Heat the oil in a wide shallow pan and cook the gammon steaks for 5–7 minutes on each side until browned. Lift out and keep warm.

3. Put the apple wedges and vegetables into the pan and stir in the stock and cider, if using, or extra stock, orange rind and juice, a little pepper, mustard and sugar. Bring to the boil, reduce the heat and cook for 5 minutes. Put the gammon back into the pan and cook in the sauce for 3–4 minutes both sides until cooked through and the sauce has reduced.

4. Spoon the vegetables onto hot plates, top with the gammon and apple and spoon over the sauce.

Venison and Juniper Cassoulet

Appears to be a lot of ingredients, but well worth the effort. A French dish of meat, sausages and beans slowly cooked for the flavours to develop. I've added a crunchy topping of mustard-topped slices of French bread.

Serves 4

500 g/1 lb 2 oz stewing venison

4 venison sausages

2 streaky (fatty) bacon rashers (strips)

8 small shallots

2 large carrots

1 small turnip

2 garlic cloves

1 orange

400 g/14 oz can haricot beans

2 tbsp olive oil

6 juniper berries

300 ml/½ pint/1½ cups game or chicken stock

150 ml/¼ pint/⅔ cup red wine or water

Freshly milled salt and black pepper

Butter

6–8 slices French bread

Dijon mustard

1. ▶ Preheat the oven to 160°C, 325°F, Fan 145°C, Gas 3. Trim the venison and cut into large bite-size pieces. Cut the sausages in half. With scissors trim the rind from the bacon and cut into small pieces. Halve the shallots if large and finely chop the carrots and turnip. Crush the garlic. Grate the rind from the orange, cut in half and squeeze the juice. Drain the beans.

2. ▶ Heat the oil in a flameproof casserole, add the bacon and shallots and cook on a medium heat for about 5 minutes, stirring occasionally until golden brown. Lift out with a slotted spoon. Add the venison pieces and sausages, in small batches, browning quickly on all sides and lift out of the pan. Put the carrots and turnip into the casserole and cook for 5 minutes.

3. ▶ Return the bacon, shallots, venison pieces and sausages to the dish and stir in the orange rind and juice, beans, juniper berries and garlic. Pour in the stock and wine or water. Season and bring just to the boil.

4. ▶ Cover, put into the hot oven and cook for 45 minutes.

5. ▶ Meanwhile, butter the bread slices and spread with a little mustard. Uncover the casserole and arrange the bread slices over the top. Cook for a further 15–20 minutes or until the venison is tender and the bread is crusty golden.

Turkey, Cranberries, Chestnut and Wheat

Pre-cooked wheat is a useful store-cupboard ingredient. Wheat has a nutty flavour. If you can't find pre-cooked, then soak the wheat in cold water or put in a pan of water and cook until tender.

Serves 4

1 small red onion
1 medium leek
200 g/7 oz Brussels sprouts
1 satsuma orange
6 cooked, shelled chestnuts
Small bunch of parsley
350 g/12 oz slice of turkey breast
1 tbsp olive oil
3 tsp chicken bouillon powder
Large handful of cranberries
250 g/9 oz pre-cooked wheat
6 sage leaves
Freshly milled salt and black pepper

1▶ Put the kettle on to boil. Halve the onion and cut into thin wedges. Thinly slice the leek and quarter the sprouts. Cut the orange in half and squeeze the juice. Break the chestnuts into pieces. Finely chop the parsley. Cut the turkey into bite-size pieces.

2▶ Heat the oil in a heavy-based pan and cook the onion and leek until softened and beginning to brown. Remove from the pan. Cook the turkey pieces until browned all over and return the onion and leek to the pan.

3▶ Pour 400 ml/14 fl oz/1⅔ cups hot water into the pan and stir in the bouillon powder, orange juice, cranberries, wheat, sage leaves and half of the parsley. Bring to the boil, reduce the heat and cook for 30 minutes.

4▶ Stir in the chestnuts and Brussels sprouts and cook for 5 minutes until the turkey is cooked through.

5▶ Stir in the remaining parsley and season if necessary. Serve immediately.

Creamy Bolognese Sauce
with Noodles

Or ragù sauce, here served with noodles, but you could spoon over hot pasta or into large Yorkshire puddings, or ladle onto baked potatoes or serve with roasted vegetables. In place of the beef, use minced lamb or chicken or turkey with chicken stock and dry white wine. For a very speedy curry, add a little of your favourite curry paste.

Serves 4

1 large onion
2 carrots
2 celery sticks
1 garlic clove
4 sun-dried tomatoes
3 sprigs of oregano
2 tbsp olive oil
450 g/1 lb lean minced (ground) beef
100 g/3½ oz pancetta
600 ml/1 pint/2½ cups beef stock
150 ml/¼ pint/⅔ cup red wine or stock
3 tbsp tomato purée
2 bay leaves
Two 300 g/10½ oz packets prepared thick noodles
150 ml/¼ pint/⅔ cup double (heavy) cream
Freshly milled salt and black pepper

1. ► Finely chop the onion and carrots, slice the celery and crush the garlic. Thinly slice the sun-dried tomatoes and pull the oregano leaves from the stalks.

2. ► Heat the oil in a large saucepan. Add the beef and pancetta and cook until browned. Lift out of the pan with a slotted spoon and put into a bowl.

3. ► Put the onion, carrots, and celery into the pan and cook until starting to brown and soften.

4. ► Return the meat to the pan and pour over all the stock. Stir in the garlic, sun-dried tomatoes, tomato purée, oregano leaves and the bay leaves. Bring just to the boil, reduce the heat, cover, and cook for 25 minutes or until the meat and vegetables are cooked through.

5. ► Stir the noodles and cream into the pan, and, stirring, cook for 5 minutes until the noodles are piping hot. Season if necessary and serve immediately.

Guinea Fowl with Thyme and Grapes

One guinea fowl generously serves two, or three small appetites, with a little bit over for sandwiches. The dark meat is slightly gamey and a cross between chicken and pheasant. This is a lovely way to cook the bird as it can be a little dry. Here it is surrounded by a layer of potatoes and onions which absorb all the flavours.

Serves 2

2 large potatoes

2 onions

6 shelled, cooked chestnuts

4 sprigs of thyme

300 ml/½ pint/1¼ cups chicken or game stock

2 tbsp balsamic vinegar

1 large guinea fowl

Freshly milled salt and black pepper

Butter, for brushing

2 streaky (fatty) bacon rashers (strips)

200 g/7 oz seedless green grapes

140 g/5 oz cranberries

1▶ Preheat the oven to 200°C, 400°F, Fan 185°C, Gas 6. Scrub and thinly slice the potatoes (leaving on the skins) and finely chop the onions. Break the chestnuts into large pieces. Pull the leaves off the thyme stalks. Stir the vinegar into the stock.

2▶ Wash the guinea fowl and dry with kitchen paper. Season both the inside and outside. Spread a little butter over the breasts of the bird and lay the bacon rashers (strips) on top.

3▶ Put the bird in the centre of a roasting time and arrange the potato slices and onions around. Pour the stock and vinegar mix over the potatoes and onions and scatter the thyme leaves over the chicken and vegetables.

4▶ Cover, put into the hot oven and cook for 40 minutes. Remove the cover and scatter the grapes, chestnuts and cranberries over the vegetables.

5▶ Cook for a further 20 minutes until the bird is golden brown and cooked through (to check, insert a skewer into the thickest part of the thigh – the juices should run clear). Cover and leave for 10 minutes to rest before carving. Scoop the vegetables and fruit onto hot plates and top with the portion of the guinea fowl.

Trout and Wholegrain Rice Fishcakes

Cornmeal gives a crisp coating to the fishcakes. Serve as a light meal with dips or put into hot buns with a little salad and pickle.

Serves 4

4 sprigs of parsley
250 g/9 oz skinless ready-to-eat smoked trout
250 g/9 oz cooked brown rice
1 tbsp tomato relish
Freshly milled black pepper
4 tbsp cornmeal
1 medium egg
Sunflower oil, for frying

1. Pull the leaves from the parsley stalks and finely chop. Flake the fish into small pieces, removing any bones.

2. Put the rice into a bowl and add the fish, parsley and tomato relish, and season with pepper. With a fork, mix together well.

3. With wetted hands, divide and shape the mixture into eight burger shapes.

4. Put the cornmeal onto one plate and break the egg onto another. Beat the egg with a fork. Use a fork and spoon to roll the fishcakes, one at a time, first in the beaten egg and then in the cornmeal. If possible chill for 15 minutes to let the coating set.

5. Heat the oil in a frying pan and over a medium heat cook the fishcakes, in batches if necessary, for 3–4 minutes either side until golden and cooked through.

Mandarin Orange, Ginger and Walnut Upside-Down Pudding

Delicious pudding for a cold winter's day, very comforting. Serve with custard, cream or crème fraîche.

Serves 6

115 g/4 oz/½ cup butter, plus extra for greasing
3 mandarin oranges
140 g/5 oz light brown caster sugar
175 g/6 oz self-raising flour
1 tsp ground ginger
2 medium eggs
2 tbsp milk
100 g/3½ oz chopped walnuts

1. Line the base of a deep 20 cm/8 inch flan tin or flat ovenproof dish with a disc of greaseproof or parchment paper and lightly butter. Preheat the oven to 180°C, 350°F, Fan 165°C, Gas 4.

2. Finely grate the rind from two of the oranges. Peel all the oranges, removing as much pith as possible, then thinly slice, removing any pips.

3. Sprinkle 25 g/1 oz of the sugar over the base of the tin and arrange the oranges on top.

4. Sift the flour and ginger into a mixing bowl. Add the butter, caster sugar, orange rind, eggs and milk. Beat until well mixed, light and fluffy then stir in the walnuts. Spoon over the oranges and smooth.

5. Put into the hot oven and cook for about 50 minutes until the sponge has risen and is firm to the touch.

6. Serve hot or warm.

Prune, Pear and Almond Pastry Slice

Crisp crunchy filo pastry is wrapped around fresh and dried fruits interspersed with pieces of almond paste. Filo pastry soon becomes dry and brittle, so keep it covered with clear film (plastic wrap) or a damp piece of kitchen paper. Serve with scoops of vanilla ice cream or pour over hot custard.

Serves 4–6

12 ready-to-eat prunes

1 small orange

100 g/3½ oz almond paste

150 ml/¼ pint/⅔ cup single (light) cream

2 medium eggs

55 g/2 oz/¼ cup soft brown sugar, plus 1 tbsp

2 pears

10 sheets of filo pastry, thawed if frozen

Sunflower oil, for brushing

4 tbsp apricot conserve

1. Preheat the oven to 190°C, 375°F, Fan 175°C, Gas 5. Oil a 20 cm/8 inch square cake tin – or a small roasting tin, or round ovenproof dish.

2. If necessary, stone (pit) the prunes and cut each into four. Finely grate the rind from the orange, cut in half and squeeze the juice. Tear or cut the almond paste into small pieces, roughly the size of a pea. Pour the cream into a jug and mix in the eggs, sugar (reserving 1 tbsp), orange rind and juice. Halve the pears, remove the stalks and cores, then thinly slice.

3. Unroll the filo pastry, keeping it covered with clear film (plastic wrap) until needed. Working quickly, brush a pastry sheet with a little oil and line the tin, leaving the excess hanging over the sides. Repeat with another six sheets of pastry, placing them at alternate angles.

4. Spread the conserve over the pastry base and arrange the prunes and pears on top, scattering over the almond paste pieces.

5. Brush the remaining pastry sheets with oil and put on top of the filling. Fold the excess pastry over, scrunching to give a crumpled look. Brush with a little oil and scatter over the remaining sugar.

6. Put into the hot oven and cook for 35–40 minutes until crisp and golden.

187

Apples and Dried Fruits with Cinnamon, Red Grape and Nutmeg Flavours

*All the flavours of mulled wine, but without the alcohol.
Serve with thick yogurt and crushed brandy snaps.*

Serves 4

3 eating apples
4 ready-to-eat dried prunes
2 ready-to-eat dried apricots
1 small orange
55 g/2 oz/¼ cup butter
3 tbsp soft brown sugar
300 ml/½ pint/1¼ cups red grape juice
Small piece of cinnamon stick
2 cloves
Pinch of grated nutmeg
Large handful of green sultanas

1. Quarter the apples, remove and discard the cores, and cut into thick wedges. Quarter the prunes and apricots. Finely grate half of the orange, halve and squeeze out the juice.

2. Melt the butter in a medium, non-stick pan and when it begins to sizzle, add the apples and cook quickly, turning them once, until golden brown on both sides. Lift out of the pan onto a plate.

3. Put the sugar, grape juice, cinnamon stick, cloves, nutmeg, orange rind and juice and dried fruits into the pan. Bring to the boil, stirring until the sugar has dissolved. Reduce the heat and simmer for 8 minutes. Return the apple slices to the pan and heat through.

4. Serve hot or cold.

Coffee, Chocolate and Walnut Bread Pudding

Luxurious pudding to share with friends, delicious on its own or with a little pouring cream, or even chocolate sauce.

Serves 4

Butter
8 slices fruited brioche bread, about 250 g/9 oz
60 g/2¼ oz plain chocolate drops
60 g/2¼ oz chopped walnuts
60 g/2¼ oz cranberries
4 tbsp caster sugar
3 large eggs
600 ml/1 pint/2½ cups milk
150 ml/¼ pint/⅔ cup strong black coffee, cold
1 tbsp grated orange rind

1. ▶ Lightly butter a shallow ovenproof dish. Generously butter each slice of bread. Cut into fingers, or squares – the size doesn't really matter.

2. ▶ Arrange half the bread pieces in the dish. Sprinkle over the chocolate drops, the walnuts, cranberries and half the sugar. Cover with the remaining bread pieces, butter side up and sprinkle over the remaining sugar.

3. ▶ In a small bowl mix together the eggs and milk then strain into a jug. Stir in the coffee and orange rind and pour into the dish. Leave to stand for 30 minutes.

4. ▶ Preheat the oven to 180°C, 350°F, Fan 165°C, Gas 4.

5. ▶ Put the dish into the hot oven and bake for 45–55 minutes until cooked and golden. Serve hot or cold.

Index